POWER IN

POWER IN 1

POWER IN THE BLOOD

POWER IN THE BLOOD

TITLE PAGE

POWER IN THE BLOOD

Copyright © Donald Simpson, 1996

All rights reserved

First published in Great Britain in 1996 by
MAINSTREAM PUBLISHING COMPANY
(EDINBURGH) LIMITED
7 Albany Street
Edinburgh EH1 3UG

ISBN 1 85158 830 2

No part of this book may be reproduced or transmitted in any form or by any means without written permission from the publisher, except by a reviewer who wishes to quote brief passages in connection with a review written for insertion in a magazine, newspaper or broadcast

A catalogue record of this book is available from the British Library

Typeset in
Printed and bound in Great Britain by

POWER IN THE BLOOD

CONTENTS

CHAPTER 1	*In the Beginning*	000
CHAPTER 2	*Revelations*	000
CHAPTER 3	*Numbers*	000
CHAPTER 4	*Judges*	000
CHAPTER 5	*Chronicles*	000
CHAPTER 6	*Acts*	000
CHAPTER 7	*Lamentations*	000
CHAPTER 8	*Exodus*	000

POWER IN THE BLOOD

1. Would you be free from your burden of sin?
   There's power in the blood, power in the blood!
   Would you o'er evil a victory win?
   There's wonderful power in he blood!

   There is power, power, wonder-working power,
   In the blood of the Lamb.
   There is power, power, wonder-working power,
   In the precious blood of the Lamb.

2. Would you be free from your passion and pride?
   There's power in the blood, power in the blood!
   Come then for cleansing to Calvary's tide;
   There's wonder power in the blood!

3. Would you be whiter, yes, whiter than snow?
   There's power in the blood, power in the blood!
   Sin stains are lost in its life-giving flow;
   There's wonderful power in the blood!

4. Would you do service for Jesus your King?
   There's power in the blood, power in the blood!
   Would you live daily His raises to sing?
   There's wonderful power in the blood!

LEWIS EDGAR JONES (1865–1936)
Reproduced by permission of
Salvationist Publishing and Supplies Ltd.

Acknowledgements

I owe especial gratitude to Sarah Campbell for her efficient proof reading and typing of the manuscript and many useful suggestions; to Harry Kent who shared the proof reading; to Jacqueline Hilley for managing to write such a balanced foreword within a very tight schedule; to David Robertson who spent many cold winter hours to obtain an atmospheric photograph of Glasgow's Kelvin Way and for the moral support of these four dear friends throughout this project.

POWER IN THE BLOOD

Foreword
Jacqueline Hilley

There have been many books written over the years claiming to have tracked down elusive killers. This book is different from the rest! Not only does author Donald Simpson shatter several misconceptions and myths but he manages to succeed in presenting the reader with a definitive, first-hand account of a man he believes has eluded the police for 25 years.

Amid the mystery and folklore of a series of crimes that have baffled many for years, emerges an explosive and original new book that promises to prise open a Pandora's box of controversy and debate. *Power in the Blood* explores the life of one man: a man the writer believes to be the infamous 'Bible John'.

On an ordinary warm and sunny August day in 1991, a gardener, tending his array of blossoms, was interrupted by a stranger. Donald Simpson, amiable and genial man, smiled at the visitor's obvious appreciation of his garden. Nothing remarkable occurred during that brief encounter, and Simpson could never have guessed that he would, in time, come to believe that the seemingly pleasant admirer was, in fact, a psychopathic murderer.

In this gripping new book, the author presents the reader with the ultimate biography of a man he suspects is a serial killer. The reader is provided with the stamp of authenticity

to a series of events that have become a media-inspired folk tale. Simpson paints a picture of religious obsession, compulsion and subterfuge in one man's holy war against the 'unclean'.

Remarkably, the story is based on the author's direct experiences and responses, which compelled him to compile a dossier chronicling a detailed account and study of John X, the man Simpson believes to be responsible for the three Glasgow murders of the 1960s. The lucid, factual dialogue and settings centre around these two central characters, who both lived in the West End of Glasgow.

As the book progresses, the reader is given an insight into Simpson's motivation and gradual conviction that John X was a fugitive, intent on going to any lengths to protect himself from the law. His suspicions were further fuelled by the sinister revelations the suspect revealed to him throughout their meetings. In his quest to find out just exactly what made this strange man tick, the writer patiently and painstakingly quizzed John X about his past life, his habits, views and beliefs. Eventually Simpson saw an emerging pattern; startling coincidences appeared as he correlated the relevant information with John X's personal history and the documented facts that were available concerning the 'Bible John' case.

In a magnetising blend of subjective and objective investigation, Simpson compared the dynamics of 'Bible John' and John X, and has put together an astonishing profile of the man he strongly suspects of not only committing the Barrowland murders but also other unsolved killings committed strategically, according to Simpson, in various parts of Scotland.

There is an extraordinary amount of factual discussion contained in the book, which occurred over the four years of

this bizarre experience. The lucid conversations between Simpson and John X serve to enrich and enhance the story's credibility. The author, a Glasgow man by birth, understands the cultural background of the man he believes to be 'Bible John'. John X, whilst responding to this empathy, allowed the writer a view into his private past; a past tormented and haunted by demons and violence.

John X emerges as a broken personality; a man struggling to survive among the two prevalent classes in the Glasgow of the sixties. Unable to live up to his middle-class aspirations, he lived in a no-man's land between the working class, where he struggled to hold on tenuously to his complex sense of superiority, whilst staring enviously from his goldfish bowl into a world he yearned to belong to, but to which he never made the grade.

Formerly a pupil at a fee-paying school in Glasgow, John X left at 16 years of age, with no formal qualifications. His only claim to respectability had its roots in a refined West of Scotland accent and his cultured manners. Unable to relate to the people he worked with, he suffered frequent breakdowns and mental health problems.

Unable to sustain relationships with women, John X's warped ideas and values found a home in religion. By resorting to biblical quotations, he justified his hatred and resentment towards the 'unclean'. The sociological and psychological implications of such a personality make for avid reading and enquiry.

If, as Simpson suggests, John X is indeed the elusive 'Bible John', the pertinent question arises: if the suspect were to resume the killings, would he be easier to detect due to today's more sophisticated information techniques, such as DNA fingerprinting and modern psychological profiling relating to serial killers?

The fascinating cultural mixture of 1960s permissiveness had a curious effect on Glaswegians. Those tempted by clandestine sexual encounters, cloaked and disguised in the trappings of forbidden romance, created a conflict of morality within themselves. Participants became actively involved in extra-marital affairs but were afraid of ultimately being discovered by their spouses.

In the context of that era the Calvinist ethics which permeated Scottish society were not an easy ethos to dissolve overnight. Glaswegians, like many people in the Western world, were undergoing a major transition. A revolution against sexual repression was in progress and was being met with fierce resistance. Both church and establishment were intent on maintaining the status quo, namely the upholding of traditional family values. these institutions berated the sixties era of accessible contraception for women, and saw this as a forerunner to the breakdown of society. In his own twisted way 'Bible John' could be considered to be one of their most staunch allies.

Simpson illustrates, meticulously, John X's aversion to adulteresses. Did this hatred initiate him into a holy war against these women? And did this self-appointed Angel of Death expedite these women as a token gesture, in a bid to halt adulterous relationships in a climate of diminishing morality? Simpson believes that one of the killer's main objectives was to humiliate his victims. The horrific manner of their deaths appears to show a deliberate attempt to shame these women, who were all strangled and left partially clothed.

Working through a minefield of cryptic clues, Simpson methodically uncovers substantial facts and circumstantial evidence. He gives the reader a concise and identifiable picture of John X and his maimed perceptions. John X,

haunted and plagued by an Old Testament morality, went to sinister lengths in his translations of biblical quotations. In selecting, among others, the Old Testament Book of Numbers, he created his own form of symbolism which served to fuel his obsessive, religious impulses. A man who, by his own admission, believed he was a divine messenger, became locked into his own fantasy version of personal morality.

One of the important questions the book poses is this: how does a civilised society resolve the dilemma of the psychopathic mind? This individual who, on a superficial level may seem quite normal, but appears to be constitutionally incapable of either knowing or feeling the difference between right and wrong, as can be witnessed in the conversations between the author and the suspect. The only remorse he seems capable of is reserved for himself, rather than for his victims.

John X's own clinical depiction of his attempt to murder his father is profoundly chilling. He typifies a sick mind who doesn't know that he doesn't know. There is no clue to his true feelings before or after he tried to strangle his father; nor does he divulge to Simpson, despite numerous promptings, just what drove him to take such a course of action. The author's conclusion is startling – he is convinced that John X would go to any lengths to silence those who knew of his crimes.

Throughout the book there is a palpable tension and gradual build-up of suspense as Simpson peals away the layers of the man he has so artfully pursued. The climax of the book is one of mind-blowing proportions. Ripping off the final layer of the mask, Simpson finally confronts John X with what he believes to be the suspects true identity.

Both author and suspect make a formidable duo – one

searching for the truth; the other hiding and perhaps incapable of facing who and what he is. If John X is, indeed, 'Bible John', the reality of his actions have been catastrophic in terms of not only his victims, but of the children who were left motherless and families who have suffered indescribable pain and grief over the loss of their loved ones.

Intriguingly, the parallels between the Peter Sutcliffe case and John X are staggering. John X admitted that the police had interviewed him three months after the Helen Puttock murder was committed, just as Sutcliffe had been interviewed concerning the 'Yorkshire Ripper' case. He told Simpson that when the police arrived he was reading his Bible. It seems permissible to ask whether the Glasgow police, like the Yorkshire police, had preconceived ideas concerning the person they were hunting. Did John X's seemingly respectable and devoutly Christian demeanour somehow cancel him out of the police enquiries.

It perhaps needs to be stressed that Donald Simpson did not, from the start, set out to write a 'sensationalised' book. In a sense the evolving story contained in this book is a testimony to the author's extraordinary experience that, perchance, took place through a casual encounter. Whatever conclusions the Glasgow police or the media reach, the reader is invited to digest Power in the Blood and come to his or her own conclusions . . .

Preface

Glasgow, like many large cities, has its quota of murders – gangland, domestic, opportunist, and street. Both in the past and in recent years some of these murders have captivated Glasgow citizens because of their special notoriety and none so much as the unsolved 'Bible John' murders which occurred in the late 1960s.

Many articles have been written on the subject, and theories expounded. Suggestions by some of the officers involved in the hunt for the perpetrator concluded that as the murders had stopped after the third victim, he had committed suicide, or that he was an expatriate who returned to kill and vanished back to his adopted abode.

The huge dragnet that had been cast failed to haul in the killer. Detective Superintendent Joe Beattie in charge of the enquiries at the time, told me: 'I always had a hunch he was right under our noses. One of my officers somewhere along the line of enquiry let him slip out of the dragnet.' Mr Beattie, an ex-World War II pilot who joined the Glasgow police after the war, had a formidable clear-up record. In his career he investigated many murders which he solved and only three were never brought to court. In two of the three he knew the killers and never had enough evidence to bring them to justice. The third and last one was 'Bible John', of whom Mr Beattie said, 'I did not even have a name to go on,

it has always bugged me, i have never let go, my search has continued even in my retirement from the police. I know my instincts were correct, someday I'll have that name.'

This story is based on the police investigations at the time of the 'Bible John' hunt. This account could prove that his instincts were correct. Did 'Bible John' commit suicide? I think not. Did he go on to kill again? I believe he did. The decision to write this book has been encouraged by ex-Superintendent Beattie who to this day, twenty-five years after the murders, has shown tenacious perseverance in continuing his search for the killer. All the clues accumulated and the individual facts, combined and form a pattern, the pattern of a serial killer. Although 'Bible John' remains at large, Mr Beattie has a name now and the case, like a fascinating jigsaw puzzle, can finally be fitted right to the last piece.

Truth is stranger than fiction, but so strange will some of the occurrences related in the following pages appear to the reader, that I deem it necessary to state that they are indeed true. I tell the story as it was related to me over a period of about four years with each new piece of information being written down by me at the time. I have not used dramatic licence to enhance the story in any way.

CHAPTER 1

In the Beginning

'Can any hide himself in secret places that I shall not see him?' sayeth the Lord.
(JEREMIAH, CHAPTER 23, VERSE 24)

A heavy frost blanketed the streets of Glasgow early on the morning of 23 February 1968 when Mr Maurice Goodman, of Carmichael Place, on the south side of the city, walked into Carmichael Lane to collect his car. As he approached his lock-up garage, which stood in a slight recess, he recoiled in horror. Lying in the recess was a naked body. He hastily returned to his home and summoned the police. First on the scene was Detective Sergeant Andrew Johnstone and Detective Constable Norman MacDonald. As they approached the body they thought it was a man, but on closer inspection realised it was a female. Their experience confirmed she had not died of natural causes and a major murder enquiry was soon in full swing with all the trappings of on-scene forensic experts, the police surgeon and photographers. The lane was taped off and a screen was placed around the body. Detective Superintendent Elphinstone Dalglish took charge of the enquiry and Police surgeon Dr James Imrie confirmed that death was due to strangulation and the markings on the victim's neck showed that a ligature had been used. She had also suffered facial

injuries which had been caused by punching or kicking to render her unconscious before strangulation. There was no trace of the woman's clothing or handbag, leading the police to speculate she may have been murdered elsewhere and the naked body dumped in the lane. A search of the immediate area for clues near the body revealed a soiled sanitary towel and a later post-mortem confirmed it belonged to the victim. It was several hours before the victim was identified.

Door-to-door enquiries revealed nothing, although a lady living nearby thought she had heard a female shout 'leave me alone' the previous night. An ambulance man said he was sure he recognised her as a nurse. The police made an immediate check at the nearby Victoria Infirmary but there were no reports of any missing persons at the hospital. Passers-by were questioned by the [police but this didn't establish anything. A thorough search of the surrounding area revealed nothing which could identify the lady.

The early editions of the evening newspapers were ox the streets shortly after lunch-time, confirming that the police were treating the whole matter as a murder enquiry. It was this publicity which finally answered the question as to who the victim was.

She was 25-year-old Patricia Docker who had a four-year-old son and had recently separated from her husband, a corporal in the RAF. She had been staying with her parents at 29 Langside Place. On the previous evening Patricia had left her parents' home telling them she was going dancing. Little did they know they were not see her alive again. She had been employed as a nursing auxiliary at Mearnskirk Hospital. Her father, Mr John Wilson, had not been too worried when she hadn't returned from the dancing as she often stayed with friends. It was when he heard that the body of a young woman had been found that he contacted the

police late in the afternoon and her identity was established. A post-mortem examination of the body was carried out by Professor Gilbert Forbes of the Department of Forensic Medicine at Glasgow University. This confirmed that Dr Imrie's original finding as to the cause of death was correct; it was clearly a case of strangulation. Another point to emerge from Professor Forbes's examination was to become significant many months later: Patricia Docker had been menstruating at the time of her death. Now that fact was merely noted at the time. There was no clear evidence of sexual assault and the police simply recorded the pathologist's finding along with the other evidence. Little did they know that within less than two years, two other young women were to be found murdered in similar circumstances, and they to would be found to be having their monthly period. Such strange coincidences were to emerge in the future.

A very attractive girl, about five feet five inches in height, of slim build and with short brown permed hair, she was a keen dancer. Had she been killed because of sexual advances tat had been rejected? Where were her clothes? Who was the person she ha met? Why was she killed? Friends were unable to assist the police. Did anyone have a motive for killing her? Was it a robbery gone wrong? Or was it revenge? It was probable that she was killed because of something that had happened within the strict confines of the night before. She had probably met he killer for the first time, then had gone willingly with him to the place of her death. Had she refused some sexual favour and thus been killed in frustration? The police now turned to Patricia's parents. They could tell the police about her background, her interests and, most importantly, where they thought she had been the night before. The Wilsons gave the police all of the information

they knew. What they couldn't say was who Patricia had been with the previous evening, nor could they account for her precise movement after she left home. But the police now had a vital lead: the Majestic Ballroom in Hope Street, and it was to this establishment that the enquiry switched.

It became more probable that she had met her killer at the dancing. That very night the police went to the dancing. It was an exercise which would be repeated many times in the coming months. They wanted to find out if anyone had seen Patricia there the night before and, above all, who was she with? had she been seen with a particular individual leaving the dance hall, then that person would be an essential witness. He might be the murderer himself. If this was what had happened, then the dancers in the Majestic Ballroom could have vital information.

The arrival of the police at a dance hall is usually to deal with trouble or fighting. That Friday, dancers were to find police officers on the band-stand. An announcement was made over the loudspeaker to anyone who had been in the dance hall the night before and they were asked to go to the foyer. Those who did so were shown a photograph of Patricia Docker and asked if they had seen her before. A man came forward to say he thought he recognised her at the majestic on the night of her death but he couldn't say who she had been with.

Meanwhile, the door-to-door enquiries in the streets surrounding Patricia Docker's home continued but no one knew of her movements, nor were they able to say what she had been doing the previous night.

Enquiries at RAF Digby in Lincolnshire, where Patricia's estranged husband was stationed, revealed that he had been on leave at the time of the murder. He was traced to his parents' home in East Lothian; they said he had been there

on the evening of the murder but had gone to St Andrews the next day. Police tracked him down there to inform him of his wife's death and on the Saturday following the murder he was brought to Glasgow to identify the body. But he could give no information as to his wife's activities the previous Thursday; in fact he had not seen her since the previous October.

There was still no sign of Patricia's clothing or her handbag. A thorough search of Carmichael Place and the immediate neighbourhood had produced nothing. The Police Underwater Unit was called in to search the nearby River Cart. Her clothing was never found, but part of the casing of her watch was found in the water was was her handbag.

Police were shocked when, weeks later, the witness who had said he'd seen her at the majestic Ballroom admitted he had not seen her at all. Weeks of police time and effort had been wasted. They had been questioning dancers at the Majestic when another more reliable witness confirmed she had been at the Barrowland Ballroom. three cars had been seen in the area late on the night of the murder. A Morris 1000 Traveller, a white Ford Consul and a foreign car, all of which were traced an cleared from the enquiry. For months the police attended the Barrowland Ballroom questioning dancers but the result was a complete blank. Detectives experienced the utter helplessness of it all, their enquiries leading nowhere. The police, in knowing there was a strangler at large in Glasgow, kept the case open and waited reluctantly to see if he would strike again. The scent of failure was in the air and so the enquiry slowly wound down.

Eighteen months later, on Monday, 18 August 1969, the body of Jemima ('Mima') McDonald was found in a derelict tenement in MacKeith Street, Bridgeton, on the east side of Glasgow. She was 32 years old, five feet seven inches in

height, with dark brown hair, and the mother of three children. She had left home two days earlier on the evening of Saturday, 16 August, to go dancing at the Barrowland Ballroom. Her three children had been left in the care of her sister, Margaret O'Brien, who lived in the same building on the same landing, their front doors facing each other. When Jemima did not return on the Saturday night Margaret was not worried. Sunday passed as she waited anxiously for her return, and by Monday morning she was very concerned. Jemima's own three children were unconcerned; there was always plenty of interest for them in the neighbourhood. but a few closes along in MacKeith Street, there stood some derelict tenements, and it was in these that a grim find was soon to be made.

Some children who had been playing on Sunday in the derelict tenement, which was only a few doors along from where the two women lived, had reported seeing a body there and no one believed them. Margaret went to the derelict tenement and found the body of her sister lying in a bed recess. She was partly clothed and had been strangled with her own tights. Detective Chief superintendent Thomas Goodall led the hunt for the killer of Jemima. There were similarities in her murder and that of Patricia Docker. Both had been to the Barrowland, they had been beaten and strangled, their handbags were missing, and they had been menstruating. Corporation dustmen arrived at MacKeith Street to sift through the heaps of rubbish piled in the back courts but Jemima's handbag was never found.

The coincidences between the two murders started to emerge. Could a maniac be stalking young women in the Barrowland Ballroom, was this the work of the same killer and had he struck again? It was established at Jemima had been to the Barrowland Ballroom.

Police issued her description to the press with an appeal for information. She was described as being five feet seven inches in height, of slim build, with dark brown dyed hair, showing traces of fair, and wearing a black dress, a white frilly blouse and off-white high-heeled shoes. Almost immediately the leads started to come in. She had been seen by a number of people at the dancing; they filled in some of the details. It transpired that she had almost definitely left the dance hall just after midnight, in the company of an unknown man. She had been seen in Bain Street near the dance hall, then seen walking along the main thoroughfare of London Road to either Main Street or Landressy Street, just yards from Bridgeton Cross near her home in MacKeith Street, arriving there at about one a.m. on the Sunday morning. The police issued a further appeal for information concerning Jemima's lost handbag: it was believed to contain hair-curlers and a headscarf.

Once more the police descended on the Barrowland. Teams of detectives spoke to all the dancers on the Tuesday following the murder, while Jemima's picture was flashed on a screen and a full description of her last movements was given. The police also promised that 'the domestic problems of witnesses would be respected', a caustic comment on the fact that many had been at the dancing while spouses and family thought they were elsewhere; the police had kept in mind the difficulty with getting information from dancers in relation to the Patricia Docker enquiry a year before. Within a week after the murder, the police had sufficient information to put together a picture of the person they wanted to interview.

Two witnesses had come forward with a definite sighting and they had a description of a man seen sitting in her company at the Barrowland. He was aged between 25 and

35, about six feet tall, slimly built, with reddish fair hair cropped short, wearing a smart suit and a white shirt. From the description police were able, with the help of the Glasgow School of Art, to compile an identikit picture of the suspect. As in the case of Patricia Docker, the police again mingled with the dancers in the hope of getting a lead or spotting Jemima's killer.

Throughout those first few weeks police activity was intense. All the standard techniques were employed, including a reconstruction of events of the Saturday night. A policewoman dressed in clothing similar to that worn by Mima McDonald retraced the path of her last walk from Barrowland 50 MacKeith Street in the hope that seeing her would jog someone's memory. she was discreetly followed by a small team of detectives who would note any information received. As feared this drew a blank. It is usually a long shot but good from the standpoint of publicity. The chances of someone rushing into a police station with a vital lead after witnessing a reconstruction are slim in the best of cases, but that fact that people do see overt police activity on the streets will again fix in their minds that a huge enquiry is being carried out on their very doorsteps. In any event, the Barrowland was the major place of entertainment for the whole area; its clientele could not fail to know what was going on.

This produced a predictable side-effect: attendances at the Barrowland dropped dramatically This had happened to a certain extent at the Majestic 18 months earlier when the police went in search of Patricia docker's killer but it had been more marked when that enquiry switched to the Barrowland. And when the police went back there a second time in connection with Mima's case, the result was almost catastrophic for the management. Two reasons for this were

apparent, one more obvious than the other. Firstly, the news that there was a murderer on the loose at the dancing kept many women at home out of fear. They had to find somewhere else to go until he was caught. But for those who were not deterred by this knowledge, a different kind of fear kept them away: fear that the fact that they had been at the Barrowland at all would become known. It wasn't that the dance hall was not convenient or popular, it was just that it had a reputation for being a good place for married people to visit for the chance of a night out. However reprehensible it might be, it was nonetheless a fact that if you wanted to meet another member of the opposite sex and didn't want your spouse to find out, then you went to the Barrowland, particularly on a Thursday. And you certainly didn't want people like policemen wandering around asking questions. Nor would you readily respond to calls for people who had been at the dancing to come forward.

This had dogged the Patricia Docker case; now it was to be repeated again. Time and again the police would hear that so-and-so had been at the Barrowland, so two officers would call at the house. Perhaps both husband and wife would come to the door. The husband would reply to the police questions: 'Me? Naw, a wisny there at all,' and then, when the wife's back was turned, he would wink conspiratorially at the policeman and add excitedly, 'Can I come down and see you – she thinks I was at the pub.' It was either that or some other alibi – the bowling club, football match, dog track or other plausible male excuse. Of course, it worked the other way, too, as the police found out. The wife would deny visiting the dancing; her alibi would be something like 'I was visiting my sister' or 'I was at my mother's that weekend', when in fact she had been for a surreptitious night out. When eventually the truth was revealed, as was

inevitable in some cases, rows and fights were the result. For the police, once again it was to be a fruitless search.

The enquiries followed a similar line to those of Patricia's murder investigation and after several months when this produced nothing, the police plainclothes team were withdrawn from the Barrowland. Little did they know that this was to be a grave mistake.

Archie Macintyre took his dog for a walk into the back court of the tenement where he lived at 95 East Street, Scotstoun, in the west side of Glasgow at about 7 a.m. on Friday, 31 October 1969. His dog sniffed around for a bit before approaching something huddled near a drainpipe. The dog started to whine and Archie took a closer look and to his horror he saw a woman's body. He tried to raise his neighbours but had no success so he hurried to a nearby telephone box and called the police.

Detective Superintendent Joe Beattie took charge of the enquiry. The body was lying against the wall of the back court to the left of the close near the bottom of the drainpipes. One of her stockings had been removed and was pulled tight round her neck leaving one of her legs bare. Bruising on her face confirmed she had been struck by her attacker. Superintendent Beattie and the other police officers attending the scene took note that the victim had been menstruating, for she had been earing a sanitary towel. But this towel was not where they expected to find it; instead it was tucked neatly under the dead woman's armpit. Was this the work of some madman?

On the railway embankment at the far end of the back court an area of grass had been flattened and Superintendent Beattie concluded there had been a chase and a struggle, the victim being stunned by her attacker and dragged to the back of the building. Her stocking had been removed and used as

a ligature to strangle her. Long blades of grass caught between her shoes and feet confirmed the scenario. Was this the work of the killer Patricia Docker and Jemima McDonald? This was given credence when the identity of the victim was known, as she too had been dancing in the Barrowland Ballroom.

Mr George Puttock who lived nearby at 129 Earl Street had seen the police activity. His wife had not come home the previous night so he approached and told the police that he was looking for his wife. Superintendent Beattie took him to the body and he confirmed it was his wife.

Helen Puttock was aged 29, a brunette, with two children. She had been dead for about seven hours. Mr Puttock told Superintendent Beattie his wife had gone with her sister Jeannie to the Barrowland Ballroom the previous night. When he interviewed Jeannie, Superintendent Beattie knew he had a very important witness. Not only had she given a good detailed description, she was able to relate many other details about her sister's killer, including most of the conversation that had taken place in the two hours he had been in their company. Police confidence rose high, as it was thought that with all the details Jeannie had given they would soon have the killer.

Jeannie recalled his hair as sandy fair to slightly red, short and tidy, and combed to one side. He was about five feet ten inches in height, with a milk and roses complexion. she had described his teeth s being small with two front teeth slightly overlapping each other and one tooth missing on the right side. He had been wearing a well-cut brown suit, suede ankle boots, a blue short and a red striped military-style tie bearing a gold crest such as you would get on a club, university or military tie. On his lapel he had a small badge which he seemed to be trying to hide as he fingered it constantly. He

was well spoken, very polite and well mannered and his accent was certainly West of Scotland. He said his name was John but Jeannie couldn't remember the surname he gave but recalled that it definitely ended in '-son'. Jeannie noticed that when she sat down between dances this well-mannered dancing partner her sister had met would stand up and move his chair back to allow room for Helen to sit. She was surprised as there weren't many in the Barrowland Ballroom who would be such a gentleman. He really was out of place with his short cropped hair and his impeccable manners. The fashion at the time dictated that men wore their hair long, making him and everything about him really out of place.

When standing he was erect and straight backed, military in movement and stance. Jeannie had been asked up to dance by another man with the name 'John' with whom she had several dances and so missed some of the conversation her sister Helen had with her John. When it was time to leave, Jeannie and Helen made their way to the cloakroom queue. Helen had only her coat to collect, she didn't have a handbag but she was carrying her red purse. When they met up in the toilet Helen told Jeannie something about her dancing partner, where he worked or lived, but she couldn't remember what it was. Jeannie changed from her dancing shoes into her boots. They met up with the two men in the foyer and Jeannie noticed that as Helen's John placed his scarf around his neck, e smoothed it down at the front and he seemed to do this with an over-practical flair, and she remembered thinking 'what a mother's boy'. She referred to his half boots jokingly and pointing to her own boots said, 'You're not the only one with kinky boots.' He didn't seem to take kindly to her remark and gave her a sullen stare.

Jeannie needed cigarettes as she had smoked the few she had in the dance hall, passing the rest to the others. But

Helen's John never smoked or offered cigarettes. When she put some money in a cigarette machine it stuck in the slot. The others gathered round to help. Helen's partner suddenly changed from being well mannered and polite, and in an angry tone demanded to see the manager. Jeannie told him not to bother about it but he became more insistent. The manager appeared and he asked him what he was going to do about this lady losing her money in the machine. The manager apologised but John persisted in a firm angry tone about the money in the machine. His tone expected obedience which made the manager angry, as John started to rhyme off things that were wrong about the premises an asking who the Member of Parliament for the area was. Helen apologised for his behaviour and the manager told them to see the assistant manager downstairs, as he was in charge of the machines.

On the way downstairs John remarked, 'My father says these places are dens of iniquity. They set fire to places like these to get the insurance money and do them up with the money they get.' Jeannie remembered he had mentioned 'mother and father' a few times in the course of the evening. It was not the usual reference that the patrons of the Barrowland would make in regard to their parents. They would refer to 'Ma and Da' or 'my Mammy and Daddy' or 'Maw and Paw'. Jeannie was to remember clearly his distinct reference to 'Mother, Father', and to dens of iniquity and a lot more about this rather weird stranger. As she chatted to her own partner Jeannie noticed Helen's partner had produced something form his pocket and was saying something to her that she apparently did not believe., as she was shaking her head. Helen's face suddenly changed to a look of surprise and acceptance when she looked at the piece of paper. what he had shown her must have been rue. Jeannie

tried to get close to see the paper but John had put it back in his pocket. 'Why can't I get to see it?' she asked.

'You know what happens to nosy folk,' said John tapping the side of his nose. What was on this paper or card Jeannie was never to know.

The two couples started for home walking a short distance to the taxi rank at Glasgow Cross. It only took them a few minutes and on the way a group of youths jeered at Helen's John because of his wee short boots. He seemed to have won Helen's confidence and Jeannie wondered if the paper he'd shown her earlier had helped to win her over. Would she allow the stranger to see her home? At the taxi rank he appeared to be agitated by the presence of Jeannie and her partner and asked the other John, 'What are you doing, are you going home now?'

'I'm going to catch the late-night bus,' he replied as he bade them goodnight and walked away as Jeannie, Helen and John number one climbed into a taxi. Jeannie asked Helen about this John: 'Is he seeing us home Where does he come from?'

'Over there,' Helen said, waving her hand in no particular direction.

The taxi set off. Jeannie was to recall most of the conversation which took place in the taxi. The journey took about 20 minutes and Jeannie was feeling uneasy about the fellow passenger. She chattered with her sister and the stranger remained sullen and aloof and when he spoke he sounded arrogant. He refused to be drawn out when asked a question and he would change the subject, or remain silent. He was annoyed that Jeannie was in the taxi and he did not try to hide it. Helen had insisted that her sister was staying and that was that. When asked where he went on holiday John said he played golf and that his cousin had succeeded

in getting a hole in one. He disapproved of married women going to the Barrowland Ballroom and talked generally of adulterous women. He mentioned something about a sister and then tried to take it back. He talked scornfully about football and the Rangers–Celtic rivalry. When asked what he did at the New Year he said he did not drink, but he prayed. He said he was agnostic and do not believe in religious nonsense. The taxi had travelled west along Argyle Street, continuing along Dumbarton Road to Partick, and then to Earl Street, Whiteinch, where Helen lived. John, however, had insisted on taking Jeannie home first. Helen had agreed to this and the taxi continued on to Kelso Street, Scotstoun, where Jeannie lived.

Jeannie was surprised when he went on to mention something about foster homes or foster children and also Moses and a woman who had been stoned or had been standing at a well. Although he was not actually quoting a particular verse or paragraph from the Bible, Jeannie, having been brought up as a Catholic, recognised it as coming from the Old Testament. John had seemed to recognise his whereabouts throughout the journey and at the point where the taxi was passing Kingsway in Scotstoun John said something bout his father or another relative having worked there and that before the high flats had been built a children's home had stood on the site.

Jeannie was becoming more and more uneasy about the stranger and to compound it all, after all the fuss in the Barrowland over the cigarettes and the money she had lost in the machine, he produced a packet of Embassy cigarettes and offered one to Helen. He had had cigarettes all the time but when Jeannie asked if she could have one he didn't reply but held out the packet and turned his face away. Jeannie helped herself, taking two or three to spite him for his mean

attitude towards her. One or two fell to the floor of the taxi but she managed to pick them u without hi noticing. Another part of the conversation she recalled was about public transport. John seemed to have a detailed knowledge of the times and fares of the buses and blue trains north of the Clyde. He said he worked in a laboratory and knew the pubs in Yoker. He also said he had plenty of money, but Jeannie did not believe that part.

As the taxi neared her home she stopped it a short distance from her street as she did not want him to know exactly where she stayed. Waving, she watched the taxi turn and head back to Earl Street. Helen was not to be seen alive again. But it was not the last time the weird stranger was seen.. A late-night bus travelling along Dumbarton Road about 2 a.m. towards the city centre picked up a man in a dishevelled state. This man had been seen shortly before walking along Dumbarton Road. A passenger on the bus noticed hat his jacket was dirty and he appeared to have a scratch below his eye. He got off the bus at Gray Street which is the stop after the Kelvingrove Art Gallery and Museum, and disappeared into the night.

Superintendent Beattie was confident that Jeannie's detailed observations and recollections of the conversations that had taken place would lead them to the killer and an early arrest. In the early days after the murder Jeannie was to be prompted to try and recall any other details she could bring to mind about their deadly escort from the Barrowland Ballroom. She recalled that he had mentioned something about someone in his family being a Salvationist which she took to mean that they had been in the Salvation Army. 'I'm sure he said it was his grandmother.' Jeannie's information was of great importance to the police enquiry and superintendent Beattie knew she was the most valuable key

witness whom he was sure would recognise the killer. The murder hunt was conducted from the Marine Police Station, Partick, and when Jeannie was taken there a poster pinned on the wall of the police station drew her attention. 'That's like him,' she said. The poster was an identikit picture of the man wanted for the death of Jemima McDonald.

The police realised the possible connection. Three young women who had all been to the Barrowland Ballroom had all been strangled. Patricia Docker and Jemima McDonald had been separated from their husbands. Helen's husband had been baby-sitting to allow her to go out dancing with her sister Jeannie. All had young children. Patricia Docker's handbag and clothes were missing when she had been found murdered and her handbag recovered later from the River Cart. Jemima McDonald's handbag was missing and now, as the police already knew, Helen Puttock's red purse was also missing. Jemima McDonald and Helen Puttock had both been strangled with their own tights and although Patricia Docker's clothes were not recovered no doubt she had been strangled with her own tights. They had all been beaten about the face, probably to render them unconscious before strangulation. The same *modus operandi* had been used on the latter two victims. The killer had used a slip knot with their tights.

A thorough search of the back court where Helen Puttock had been found revealed a single cufflink. It was a cheap metal cufflink and none of the residents in the building recognised it as being his own. Police believed it belonged to the killer. Helen's purse was never found. The cufflink revealed no fingerprints but it was hoped to find one to match as it was now obvious that all three murders were the work of the same killer.

The biggest manhunt and murder enquiry that Glasgow

and Scotland had ever known was in full swing. Superintendent Beattie knew it was imperative to make an arrest quickly while the trail was still hot. He was aware that this man could kill again and he knew from experience that the first few days of an enquiry were vital. When an enquiry went on to a week and beyond into two weeks, the rail would be getting colder for the well-spoken killer who quoted from the Bible and who the press were to dub 'Bible John'. With her detailed description, Jeannie helped the police to make up a second artist's impression. This was done by Lennox Paterson, he artist who had made up the first impression. Jeannie was delighted. It was the exact likeness of the man she had been with in the company of her sister, Helen.

The other John who had been in their company at the Barrowland Ballroom never came forward. He had said that he was from the Castlemilk area of the city and appeals for him to contact the police went unheeded. His reasons were probably due to the fact that he was married and did not want his wife to find out that he had been to the dancing without her knowledge. He was not a suspect, as the police had established through the victim's sister Jeannie that it was the work of one man. The murder team of 50 detectives were ordered to leave no stone unturned and to 'find this man before he kills again'. All hospitals, psychiatric and general, in Glasgow were checked to establish whether any of their patients had been on weekend leave or had been discharged. The hospitals were asked to confirm the whereabouts of such patients on the night of the murder. Ships that sailed from Glasgow directly after the murder were located and the crews questioned and eliminated from the enquiry. Servicemen in the Army, Navy and Air Force on leave at the time were traced and questioned. Many people who resembled 'Bible John' were to submit to being questioned

and placed on identity parades. Young men between the ages of 25 and 35 who had in recent years moved from or lived in Earl Street where Helen Puttock lived, were traced and eliminated from the hunt. Over 450 hairdressers were visited in the Glasgow area and shown the identikit picture of 'Bible John'. All were asked if they recognised any customer who had similar hair colouring which had been cut to the particular short style of the suspect. The enquiries drew a complete blank.

Superintendent Beattie thought the short style of the suspect's hair could indicate that he may be or have been in one of the branches of the armed forces. If this was correct, the person he was looking for was probably an NCO – a corporal or sergeant. He probably was not a commissioned officer: he was not quite as educated or refined. The incident in the Barrowland over the cigarette machine when his bearing had changed from being quiet and well spoken to being confident and aggressive, had the stamp of a man who might have been used to ordering people around. There was another possible link with the services: was the card or paper he had shown Helen Puttock in the Barrowland a military identification document? The co-operation fro the services was overwhelming but again it led nowhere. The overlapping front teeth Jeannie had described sent detectives on the arduous task of checking all dental surgeries in the Glasgow area and Superintendent Beattie had a set of false teeth made at the Glasgow Dental Hospital, identical to the suspect's teeth. Photographs of the dentures were circulated to ever dentist in Britain. It was to no avail.

'Bible John's' suit led police to check all of Glasgow's 240 tailors in the hope that a tailor would recognise him as a customer. Again the police drew a blank.

After four months of intensive detection work the trail

was growing cold and Superintendent Beattie decided on a new line of enquiry: the occult. Dutchman Gerard Croiset, a world-famous clairvoyant, had had spectacular achievements in tracing missing persons – he was no fake. Joe Beattie had heard that Croiset was in Scotland and he was asked to assist in Glasgow. But Croiset knew nothing of the suspect or his victims when he was asked to help in the case.

The *Daily Record* newspaper set up the experiment. Without prompting he drew pictures from his mind of the area where he thought 'Bible John' might be found. Croiset thought the killer was still in Glasgow and when shown a map, indicated an area to the south-west of the city in the general direction of Govan. He then went into detail, sketching out shops, schools, recreation grounds and factories; he predicted that in this area there would be second-hand or old cars near a large engine just off a main road: and he drafted out descriptions of two shopkeepers and a customer – an elderly man who, said Croiset, knew something about the murder. What had surprised the police was the description of what Helen Puttock had been doing on the night of her death, for Croiset was able to say without prompting that she had spent her last evening dancing and how she had left in the company of some friends. There was no way that Croiset could have known this before coming to Glasgow.

Another quite separate side of the story is an interesting theory put forward by Norman Adams in his book *Goodbye, Beloved Brethren*. According to Adams, 'Bible John' might have been a member of the Exclusive Brethren. Adams points out that in addition to carrying out enquiries into all the churches and chapels in the Glasgow area, the Glasgow police also questioned families belonging to the sect in

Central Scotland. It appears also that the murder caused comment and speculation among the Exclusives at the time. Adams goes on to suggest that if 'Bible John' was a member of the sect, then the harsh teachings and measures he would have sustained in the sect could have manifested themselves in murder, presumably out of a perverse desire to rid the world of the unclean. Adams implies that the mental torture suffered by some members of the Exclusives could lead to extremely depraved behaviour and that the balance of their mind had become disturbed. Adams failed to note that 'Bible John' may have joined the Brethren as an adult with an already disturbed mind. In the book *Bible John*, by Charles Stoddart, Mr Stoddart points out that if one area in the enquiry was overlooked it was there within the Brethren. The suspect in this story was in the Brethren and later joined the Pentecostal Church.

For many years Superintendent Beattie had been on friendly terms with Dr Robert Brittain, probably Scotland's most distinguished psychiatrist. One of his specialist fields of study had been of those individuals who could be labelled sadistic psychopathic killers, many of whom Dr Brittain had assessed and diagnosed in hi professional career. He and Joe Beattie had discussed the 'Bible John' case informally on a number of occasions and, when it was suggested that Dr Brittain prepare a word description of the man the police might be looking for, the doctor readily agreed. The paper was entitled *The Sadistic Murderer* and was derived from over 20 years of experience in forensic pathology and forensic psychiatry. The description to the form of a list of characteristics commonly found in sadistic murderers. The full article appeared under the same title in a professional journal and part of it is printed in Chapter 5 of this book.

Among the features suggested by Dr Brittain, perhaps the

most interesting was that the individual concerned is commonly introspective and rather withdrawn: he is a bit of a loner, finding difficulty in relating to those around him and has a great deal of insecurity. He can, however, be vain and egocentric without displaying the gregariousness commonly associated with those traits. He is without conscience, although he may express regret for his crimes. His sexual life is usually concentrated in his mind; he is often impotent and lacking in virility, although his fantasy life is extensive. He is excited by violence, may collect weapons and spends a lot of time reading and fantasising about atrocities. The violence used in his crimes is often extensive: he kills in a state of frenzy and usually by asphyxiating his victims, after having carefully planned his crime in advance. When he has finished, he feels a great sense of relief and satisfaction. According to Dr Brittain, the sight of suffering can inflame such an individual and his brutality can be increased by the helplessness and fear of his victim, while slowly strangling a victim gives him a feeling of god-like power over life and death.

Joe Beattie took Dr Brittain's report seriously. On reading it in full, a grim picture is found in which are depicted many traits which fit the information about the suspect already known to the police. However, the major police enquiry which had been mounted with the utmost vigour slowly wound down as detectives were diverted by other pressing crimes, only to be momentarily revived when an occasional telephone call or new lead came in. Twenty-five years have passed and the only monument which now remains is a mountain of documents stored away in Police headquarters and bulging press files on the case in all the newspaper offices.

Many articles have been written on the subject since then.

Suggestions by some of the police officers involved in the hunt for 'Bible John' concluded that as the murders had stopped after the third victim, he had committed suicide. Another was that he was an expatriate who returned to kill and vanished back to his adopted abode.

POWER IN THE BLOOD

CHAPTER 2

Revelations

'How long, O Lord, holy and true, dost thou not judge and avenge our blood on them that dwell on the earth.'
(REVELATIONS, CHAPTER 6, VERSE 10)

I have always kept a lovely garden stocked with roses, hanging baskets, sweetpeas. Those of you who love flowers or gardening will understand if you have ever kept such a garden near a main thoroughfare how many people stop to admire it, unaware how very distracting it can become as you endeavour to tend it. There are bonuses though; you get to know lots of people and make friends. Some are very interesting people with their own tale to tell. Second to my love of gardening is my interest in people and I have spent many an hour chatting at the garden gate to those who dallied. Some have remained friends and others are etched in my memory. The garden I refer to is situated in a leafy suburb in the West End of Glasgow. I have since moved to a quiet, remote cottage 100 miles away in the West of Scotland.

The approach by one person in particular out of the many in that Glasgow suburb drew my attention more than any. It was a lovely sunny July day in 1991 as I was weeding a flower bed when a stranger by the gate remarked on the floral display. Work stopped again as I chatted amiably with

the friendly stranger who told me he had often meant to stop and chat. He was in his late fifties, well spoken and very articulate, and went on to tell me that he lived close by. This surprised me as I had been living there for eight years and had never seen him before. I noted his smart appearance, suit, collar and tie, and well-polished shoes, straight backed and a full head of grey hair, combed to one side. We chatted about things in general and he then went on to tell me he was a Born Again Christian and quoted some passages from the Bible, and he referred to a biblical garden, the Garden of Gethsemane. 'My name is John X,' he told me. I shook hands with him as he took his leave.

Two weeks later, on a fine sunny evening after a good day's fishing on Loch Fyne, I was sitting in my garage with a friend when he passed by and I invited him in. I asked him if he would like a glass of whisky, but he declined, saying he did not drink, and when offered a cigarette he said he didn't smoke. He did not have much to say but he listened as my friend and I talked about the adventure of our day fishing. When asked if he had ever been fishing he replied he had not but that it reminded him of Jesus because Jesus was a fisherman. We chatted on for about an hour when, suddenly, after a swear word had been used, he stood up and marched out of the garage stating that the conversation was not his cup of tea. `My friend and I looked at each other and I said that he really must be a devout Christian. I was not offended by his sudden departure at the use of the swear word as I thought it was his right to leave if he felt the conversation was in any way offensive.

A week later, I was seated in the garage wit another friend when he passed. Once more I called him in and after half an hour when a swear word unintentionally came into the conversation he again stood up and marched out of the

garage stating that his Christian beliefs could not allow him to remain. If he had left quietly, excusing himself from the company which was friendly and not offensive, I would have understood his wishes but his abrupt departure caused me to remark when he had gone that he was sanctimonious. I believe in 'live and let live' so the well-spoken Christian was not banished from my premises or from my company and I was to see him at the shops and in passing over the next few weeks and exchange brief conversations with him.

Early in the evening about the Middle of October 1991 as I was parking my car in the garage driveway I caught sight of him coming out of the off licence which was next to my home. He was blind drunk. I waited by my gate until he reached the steps leading from the shopping centre as I did not want to miss this sight. Calling to him I asked, 'What is the celebration for?' He replied drunkenly, 'Fuck the Pope!'

'There's certainly quite a change in your demeanour since I saw you last,' I said. He laughed and laughed and the smell of alcohol from his breath wafted to my nostrils in the cold evening air. He leaned right into my face laughing, and for the first time I noticed his teeth. They were the tiniest teeth I had ever seen in a man and although they were false teeth, the dentist who made them would have copied the size of his original teeth.

He leaned drunkenly against the wall by the steps and said, 'Are you for a drink? Are you inviting me into your home for a few wee drams?' His face was contorted and flushed in a drunken leer and he produced a packet of Embassy cigarettes and asked for a light. Here was a man who over several months had convinced me he was a non-smoking, non-drinking Christian who had shown offence at the slightest swear word and who could teach me to swear. Most people would have chased this character when they

discovered this transformation. I excused myself from his company then, but I was determined that I would get to know what made this man tick. There was something about him – his earlier approach as a Christian had been put forward convincingly.

Several months passed and it was not until April 1992 that I saw him again. We met in the street and I remarked that I had not seen him for some time and he told me had had had a nervous breakdown due to reading the Bible too much and had been in hospital for eight weeks. I made no mention about his drunken state on our last meeting as I thought he probably could not remember. From time to time over several weeks I met and conversed with him in the street. He was back to his Christian attitude and told me he was seriously considering studying for a degree in divinity and joining the church of Scotland as a minister. Being a gardener I was in my garage most evenings, especially in the early spring as I kept my seedlings there before planting them out. Friends and neighbours would call in to exchange interests or sit and talk. Towards the end of April 1992 I was in the garage in the early evening when he appeared again. This time he produced a half bottle of whisky and proceeded to share it with me. Engaging him in conversation I observed an individual whose company then was not in the least objectionable. He told me he was receiving invalidity benefit and that he was not working and this bothered him – he felt he had lost his self-esteem. I chatted to him for a couple of hours and he said he had enjoyed the company. When he was leaving I told him to call again.

The following evening I decided to pay him a surprise visit. I thought it was only fair to pay him back for sharing his whisky which had been purchased from his meagre income. I had taken a bottle of whisky and he made me

welcome and we settled down to chat. His conversation, ranging from current affairs to his own views on life in general, was not disjointed and was put over in an intelligent manner. As he spoke I took in the surroundings. His accommodation was comfortably furnished and consisted of a sitting-room, kitchen and bathroom; a single person's accommodation. Behind him was a bookcase which contained a couple of hundred books. I could read the titles and, being an avid reader myself, I saw every one of them was on religion. Books on Christian theology, several books of the Bible, the Old Testament, the New Testament, religious pamphlets, and a German Bible, *Die Bible*. You would expect to find such books in a priest's or minister's study and they were somehow strangely odd in these surroundings. Four library books lay on a side table and they were books on battles and i was struck by the incongruity of everything about this man.

Whether it was due to the effects of the whisky I could not say, but he stopped talking and covered his face with his hands and sobbed quietly. I waited until he had composed himself then asked what was bothering him. 'I have never told anyone about this, but I used to beat my father,' he told me.

I asked him why this had happened and he remained quiet for a few minutes. He went on to relate how he had beaten his father on several occasions and how on two occasions his father had been so severely beaten he had had to be hospitalised. 'In fact I tried to kill him,' he said, and I could sense by his expression that he expected my reaction. I asked if his father was senile or abusive to him as I had been in such a situation with a senile elderly relative who had been very trying over four years. 'No, he was not senile, but I could tell by the way he was looking at me what he was

thinking, and that is why I beat him.'

'Was your father taunting you?' I prompted.

'No, it is as I told you, I knew what he was thinking just by the way he looked at me.'

I asked him, 'How old was your father when this took place?'

'He was 78,' he replied.

'Was your mother present when you beat him?' I asked him.

'Yes, she knew I had beaten him, but on the two occasions when he was admitted to hospital my mother was in hospital herself at the time.'

'And how did you try to kill your father?' I queried.

'I had beaten him by punching him and he was lying on the floor. I took a rope and using a slip knot I attempted to strangle him. It was a miracle because the slip knot became untangled; it should not have – it did not untangle on previous occasions.'

'What occasions?' He looked flustered momentarily before he continued.

'Just as I've told you,' he said.

'What happened when he was taken into hospital?' I continued.

He replied, 'On the last occasion the police came to see me and warned me that i was lucky as my father would not bring charges against me.'

I looked at him in silence. I was trying to equate in my mind the reasoning behind this odd revelation. 'You said your mother had been present on some occasions when this took place. What was her reaction?'

'Oh, she did not say anything,' he replied. 'I just know that my father's mere presence judged me.'

I watched him as he spoke and he was calm and sort of

matter of fact in his expression. There was a pious ring to his last sentence and I wondered what father he was referring to.

'In fact my father did not come home after the last beating I gave him. The social work department placed him in an old folk's home where he remained until his death in 1983.'

'When did this take place?' I probed.

'It was in 1978 and I had tried to put him into care. At my prompting he was taken into hospital for two weeks to be assessed but the doctors and social workers said they could find nothing wrong with him and he was returned home. My mother had by then been hospitalised and I knew by the state of her mind that she would not be coming out again.'

'But why did you try to put him into care if there was nothing wrong with him?' I asked.

'I wanted him out of the house where I was staying. If I could get my father into care then I could apply to the council housing department for an exchange.' This was explained to me without feeling, as if it was a normal occurrence and he appeared totally unaware of the callousness of his actions.

'Had you always stayed with your parents and did you ever marry?' I pressed.

'No, I have never married and I have always stayed with my parents,' he replied.

'Do you have any brothers or sisters?'

'Two sisters, but they are married and do not live in Glasgow.'

He was seated with his array of religious books behind him and his inoffensive manners and tone of voice and his appearance gave him a priest-like aura. His mannerisms were definitely imitating those of a priest or minister. I visualised him with a clerical dog collar and he could have slotted into the role perfectly well. I wondered why he was

revealing his story to me. I put the question to him and he said he had never really spoken a great deal to anyone about his life for at least twenty years.

'Where were you and your parents staying before you moved here?'

'We stayed in Earl Street, Scotstoun. As soon as my father was taken into care I immediately applied for an exchange as that home held too many bad memories for me. I moved out to come and live here in 1981.'

I sensed there was more to the story than he cared to admit and I tried to prompt him further on the subject but he would not elaborate on it. I told him that maybe the beating of his father was not called for, to which he admitted that he did not know why he beat him so severely. 'I just do not know why I beat him; it just happened and I have wanted to tell someone about it.'

He told me that he was born in Partick, in Glasgow, and moved to Earl Street in Whiteinch with his parents a few years before World War II. After primary school he was accepted at a fee-paying school in Glasgow. He left at the age of 16. For a couple of years he worked as an office boy before enlisting in the RAF at the age of 18 in the early 1950s. He served for six years in the Pay Corps in the RAF, attaining the rank of corporal and left for health reasons in 1959.

He described settling into civvy life again as very difficult and he spent almost a full year at home with his parents, sinking into a deep depression, unable to go out and mix with people. This was to lead to his being hospitalised for almost a year in Crichton Royal, Dumfries, suffering from a severe nervous breakdown. When he returned home he said he sensed the minute he arrived that his mother had rejected him.

Working mainly in offices for several companies he was unable to hold down a job for long as he felt he could not relate to his work colleagues. He had always had an interest in Christianity and he described how his inconsistency at work also matched his inconsistency with Christianity. About 1963 he joined the Brethren and had also started work with Rolls-Royce as an auditor and vie years later in February 1968 he left Rolls-Royce and travelled north to Peterhead to work as an unpaid lay preacher in the Pentecostal Church, returning to Glasgow four months later. He then found work as an insurance agent and worked in that capacity until late 1969. His round covered the West End of Glasgow starting at Yorkhill then on to Hillhead, back down to Partick and along Dumbarton Road out to Whiteinch, Scotstoun, Yoker and up as far as Drumchapel. I asked him if he had had a car to cover such an extensive round and he said he travelled by public transport and knew all the times of public transport really well.

When I got home later that evening my thoughts were troubled as I mulled over what he had told me about his background. I tried to analyse the beating of his father and could not understand his reasons for doing so. There was more to this man than met the eye. I had an uncanny feeling about him that I could not shake off. Call it intuition or whatever but over the next few days my thoughts went back to that conversation. Something told me that maybe his father knew something about him, hence the violence towards his father. Then the thought came to me; the quoting of the Bible when I first met him at my garden gate that recalled in my mind the 'Bible John' murders. Could it be that his father knew he was the killer? Was it possible that 21 years since the murders I could have met 'Bible John'? I dismissed the thought as being over-imaginative but I found

my thoughts preoccupied over the next few weeks with the idea and could no put it out of my mind. A book from the library on the murders determined that I would try to find out more about John X.

* * *

My approach had to be careful without arousing suspicion and I planned to make it over a lengthy period. Too many questions asked in a short time would put him on his guard. As already mentioned, I was frequently in my garden and garage and this was to be the spider's web. If he was the killer then he would be as deadly as the spider, so I had to spin the web with intricacy. He visited often and I made him welcome. Gradually I gained his confidence, learning more about him. He was a loner and did not have any friends. For weeks at a time he was a devout Christian who now and then quoted from the Bible. This was followed by weeks without mention of any religion. I studied his appearance, his hair was always cropped short, and he dressed smartly at all times, and was always well spoken. When he spoke about his parents, which he often did, he always said 'mother' and 'father'. Jeannie, the last victim's sister, had told the police that that was how the killer referred to his parents, but at that time many people referred to there parents in such a way. There was much more about him I had to find out. His benefit, which he collected once a week, was spent mostly on drink and backing horses. It was on these pay days that I never saw him. As the months passed I was to learn of his habits which so totally contradicted his piousness. I never challenged his hypocrisy as by now I knew his piety was a disturbed part of his mind. He was always polite but became withdrawn when others joined the company. What I discovered about this man over the next two years was to be

very revealing.

I am sure a murderer using the guise of a holy man would have caused his intended victims to be off guard, unaware of what was to come. In fiction the clergyman is seldom the murderer – as Shakespeare said, 'the devil can cite scripture for his purpose'. Many clerics over the centuries have been responsible for hideous crimes. If there is a hell then I'm sure if you go there you will not be able to get near the fire as there will be so many holy men crowded round it. An evil man using the Bible can be very formidable. I decided to study John X more closely and was determined that he would not catch me off guard as i saw through his guise. After several visits to the Mitchell Library, where I read old newspapers and a couple of books on the 'Bible John' murders, I was now familiar with the known clues relating to the killer. How I was to question and match them to the suspect turned out to take longer than I imagined. There was plenty of time and I was in no hurry. As the weeks and months rolled by I looked hard and long and, careful not to delude myself, I was able slowly to extract information that matched the killer.

The first piece in the puzzle I had to establish was the hair colouring that Jeannie had described. John X's hair was now grey with no hint of the colour it had been. Asking him outright what colour his hair had been may have put him on the alert. The style of his hair fitted, it was combed to the one side and cropped short. It was a full head of hair and for his age there was not the slightest sign of it receding.

On an early summer afternoon, when I was sitting in my garage, he arrived jacketless with his shirt sleeves rolled up, and as we sat talking the sun shining on his bare arms showed up reddish, fair hair. This was my opportunity to put the question to him. 'I see you had red, fairish hair when you

were younger.'

He half smiled in surprise saying, 'How do you know that?' and I pointed to his forearms.

'Yes, you are right, my hair was that colour,' he replied.

'When did your hair start going grey?' I asked casually.

'Oh, it started to go grey in the early seventies,' he said.

I decided that this would be the way to broach future questions; I would wait for the opportunity. John X had a definite resemblance to the police identikit picture and although many years had gone by his facial features were very similar, although more lined. He wore glasses and had a thin moustache and when I sketched them in pencil onto the identikit picture the result was startling. The identikit picture became almost exactly as if it were a photograph of him, the man I had now befriended. Patience is a virtue which was to be proved as the many meetings in that garage afforded the opportunities to study him.

Several weeks later, ensconced in my garage in the early evening, I was filling in a football coupon when he arrived. It was perfect timing; it gave me the opportunity to talk about sport. 'I do not follow football,' I told him as i selected my crosses on the coupon. I did follow rugby, boxing and snooker. I asked him if he was a football supporter and he replied that he was not.

'What sports are you interested in?' I asked him, and he replied 'None.'

'Surely you have played some sport at one time?'

'Well, yes, I have played golf,' he replied. 'It is the only sport I have had an interest in.'

'When did you start playing golf?' I asked.

'Do you recall that I told you that I was in Crichton Hospital? Well, there was a golf course attached to the hospital and that is where I first played.'

'Did you continue playing when you left the hospital?' I queried.

'Yes, I have often played on Knightswood golf course,' he replied.

'Have you ever managed a hole in one?' I continued.

'No, but I have a cousin who is an all-round sportsman who has excelled in many sports and he has an array of trophies and medals to prove it; and he had a hole in one.'

I had to compose myself and act naturally. I was almost speechless and had to force myself to continue talking and appearing unperturbed but my thoughts were elsewhere. The weird stranger in the taxi had told Jeannie and her murdered sister this same story. I was shaken but I managed to hide it quite well. I had no more probing questions to ask that night so I would await my chance for the next question some other day. I had deliberately raised the question about golf, and had answered it in full. Had I caught him unaware or was it coincidence? At times he was painfully shy and I had to put him at his ease. There were times when he did not show up for many weeks and I would wonder if he had caught on to my probing. He explained the reason for his long absences was that he felt he was out of his depth, because I lived in a large property which I owned, whereas he lived in a humble council flat.

His attitude reflected a deep-seated insecurity which may have had its origins in his days at the fee-paying school. He was a boy from a council room and kitchen in Whiteinch and his father had unwittingly forced him into this affluent middle-class school. The other pupils would have teased him, as children can be cruel and he would suffer again when his pals in the neighbourhood chanter 'snob'. He had not been the scholar his parents expected. Though capable and clever he was never able to fulfil his potential and ultimately

left school with no formal qualifications. It had left him with one asset, a refined West of Scotland accent.

Putting him at ease was important and I managed to gain his confidence to the extent that he would call two or three times a week. He was eager to talk about his background and I was eager to listen. He told me a great deal about his mother with whom he said he had a love-hate relationship, describing his mother as mad. He told me that his mother was the reason he had never married and he hated women because his mental debility had been inherited from his mother. He told me his lengthy stay in Crichton Royal Hospital, Dumfries was because had had been born with all her mad traits. His two older sisters took after his father and never suffered from depression or nervous breakdowns. They had married in the late 1950s, settling down quite well. This was the only reference he made to his sisters. His father had worked at Albion Motors for many years and left to work for another company in Renfrew. At this point I reminded him that he had worked for Rolls-Royce in Hillington which meant he and his father would cross on the Renfrew ferry to get there. He agreed that that was the route, but he did not travel with his father in the morning as his father left for work earlier. 'Sometimes I would meet my father on the ferry on the way home and we would have a pint of beer in a pub in Yoker. Even if I did not meet him I would have a pint by myself in one of the Yoker pubs,' he said.

On his jacket lapel he wore a small blue and gold badge which he had a habit of fingering and I asked him what it was and he said it was a Christian fellowship bade he had been given in the mid-1960s when he had joined the Pentecostal Church. in Montague Street, just off Woodlands Road in the West End of Glasgow. I encouraged him to tell

me more of his association with this sect. Since his teens, he told me, he had attended gospel halls and many churches and it was only then that he found a church whose teachings suited him. He went on to say: 'In fact, before I found this church, I visited every church in the Glasgow area in my search for Christian conviction.' I put it to him that there were maybe 300 or even 400 churches in the Glasgow area and it would be quite an undertaking to visit each of them in turn. He went on, 'Over a period of about three years I visited a different church each week. Sometimes I would attend the Sunday morning service in one church and the Sunday evening service in another and this enabled me to cover a great deal of churches in that period.'

I had never heard of anyone attempting such an undertaking and I listened to him in astonishment. 'What was the driving force?' I continued.

'I believed I was a divine messenger of God, and it was He who had sent me on this quest. In each church I felt especially elated if the minister mentioned in the service, "God is here", I felt he was referring to me and that is what gave me the constancy to continue the search. I started in the south of the city, then east, west and north, covering as many churches as possible: until I found the church in Montague Street where the Pentecostals worshipped. Their teachings, though harsh, suited what I had been seeking.'

Extraordinary indeed, and I awaited his revelations on every visit he made to my garage over the months and I was not to be disappointed. I did not have to put direct questions as he answered a great deal without prompting. He enjoyed a drink and I made it available as it helped loosen his tongue. I played Pavarotti and Joseph Locke and other classical music on a hi-fi kept in the garage which suited his musical tastes. This eventually culminated in many disturbed

evenings for my direct neighbours.

To the casual observer he would come across as an inoffensive, introspective, very likeable character who, I have to admit, I grew to be fond of. He was always well dressed in a suit, collar and tie or sports jacket and flannels. But I knew that, like a double-edged sword, he had two sides to him. He told me how he could never maintain the standards of dress that his mother provided for him. All his clothes, he told me, from his teens up until shortly before his mother went into hospital, had been paid for out of her account at Goldbergs in Candleriggs, in the city centre. He was a man who was very vain about his dress. It was the subject of ties that gave me the cue to talk about the various styles in the late sixties and seventies, such as various clip-on psychedelic ties. He told me he had a favourite tie in the late sixties; it was a clan tie with the clan crest and was dark blue with red stripes. He said he liked that particular tie and wore it often to the dancing as it drew attention from his dancing partners who would ask him if it was a military or university tie.

He did not talk about himself all the time. We would have a drink, play music and talk on many other subjects over the months and i tried to avoid giving him an inkling of what I was trying to establish. Friends and neighbours would also be present on occasions and this helped to make him feel accepted. I discovered he had a strange modesty. I kept a bucket in the garage for urinating in as it was quite a haul to go all the way to my house and upstairs to the loo, so if any of the lads visited they would use it if need be and it was an easy matter to swill it down the drain and rinse it out. But Paterson wouldn't use it, not in front of the lads. He would trail all the way to his own house just to have a piddle and then return to the garage. He was also reluctant to use the loo

in my house. This behaviour was odd.

Sometimes we would over-imbibe on the whisky and play the hi-fi rather loud. This had drawn the attention of the neighbours, resulting many a chiding from my wife. At all costs I determined to entertain John X and keep him talking. It was after one such session I remarked about dens of iniquity and it was the first time in many years he had heard the expression. His positive responses were becoming more than a coincidence. It was so uncanny that at times I had the feeling he knew what I was doing and was maybe leading me on or else, simply through his unguarded responses, was revealing his involvement in the murders. I led him on to talk about his dancing days and he said he had often been to the Barrowland Ballroom. I asked if he went with friends, but he said he always went dancing on his own.

One evening he related a story about a visit to his sister who lived in a small town to the south of Glasgow. When he boarded the bus to return home he discovered that the money he had in his pocket wasn't enough to get him right home, so he had to get off the buss about three miles from the city centre. This meant that he had to walk from the south side all the way home to the West End, but it wasn't the first time he had had to do so. Some years previously, in the early hours of the morning, he had walked the same route. He had told this story as part of a general conversation. Aware that the first victim, Patricia Docker, had been murdered in the south side of the city, I asked him casually if he knew that part of the city well. He suddenly became very indignant about the question and angrily demanded why I had asked about the south side of the city and why I had brought it into the conversation in the first place. I was surprised by his outburst and I had to remind him that it was he who had broached the subject and not I. There was something

strangely distant in him as he glared at me and I knew he had lost the thread of his story. He was disturbed; I had touched a raw nerve.

The end of September arrived with colder evenings and it was only then that I first invited him into my home. He did not have television and he enjoyed many evenings watching ours. We had two lounges so i was able to continue observations without disturbing my wife. He and I were seated in the large lounge as my wife entered the room. On her entrance I watched as he stood up – a real gentleman. Later that evening, as he was leaving, he placed his scarf round his neck and smoothed it with exaggerated care before putting on his coat. My wife was aware of the purpose of my interest in John X but I knew that initially she did not take me seriously. She would often pop in to say hello, and he always stood up immediately, slightly moving the armchair to make sure her entrance was not obstructed. It was not casual, but military, in an old-fashioned style of chivalry. I had asked my wife to observe when he was leaving the way he smoothed his scarf. Most people straighten a scarf before donning a coat but this was a meticulous smoothing of his scarf that you could not help noticing. It was almost irritating the way he did it – a real 'mother's boy'. I asked him if his parents were religious and he replied, 'No, they were not, but my grandmother was in the Salvation Army.' He continued, 'My father and I were at her bedside when she died; I was very close to her and was very grieved on her death.'

One night we were watching a documentary on television about prostitutes during World War II. The elderly women who were being interviewed were giving their reasons why they had become prostitutes. From the corner of my eye I could see John X becoming more and more agitated. He was on the edge of his seat with an intense expression of seething

hatred on his face. I could see him clenching and unclenching his fists, the whites of his knuckles showing through. his mild-mannered composure gone. He was having great difficulty keeping control. I could see that if he could have dragged those women from the screen he would have strangled them, there and then. It was distinct Jekyll and Hyde transformation – his face had become the mask of a fiend. When the programme ended I could see it took him some time to regain his composure. I immediately put it to him that here was something about prostitutes that disturbed him.

He tried to change the subject but I persisted with the question. For several minutes he sat in stony-faced silence, then suddenly he related a peculiar story. 'For a couple of years, between 1965 and 1967, I used the services of prostitutes in the red light districts of Glasgow. I met a prostitute from Aberdeen of whom I grew very fond. I stopped using the services of the other prostitutes and only went to her. She had a distinct quint in one eye, and the last time i saw her she had had the quint corrected. I thought she had had it corrected for me. Shortly after that she disappeared and although I searched for her I never saw her again. I took it very badly; it disturbed me mentally for a long time afterwards.'

'But why do you still have this intense hate?' I continued.

'They should be married – if they found a husband they would not have to sell their bodies,' he said.

'Maybe they were married,' I suggested.

'Worse still,' he replied with deep venom in his voice.

I asked him, 'Did you ever at any time have a girlfriend?'

'At one time there was a bus conductress, who I am sure fancied me, but it sort of died.'

'Did you ask her out?' I continued.

'No, it is as I told you, it died,' he replied with an indication of finality on the subject.

My interest in this man, who alternated between quoting the Bible and drinking heavily, was being fuelled as each day passed. One of the books I had read on the murders mentioned that the murdered girl, Helen Puttock, had worked as a bus conductress. I wondered if his remarks about the conductress had been a cryptic reference to Helen. I had observed that he was capable of clever metaphor and his confidence in this led to conceit. He thought he was walking on a thick oak floor, but little did he know my discernment was reducing it to very thin ice.

A few days later at the shopping centre, while sitting in my parked car, I spotted John X in the off-licence,. When he came out I could see he was unsteady on his feet. It was the day he cashed his social security book. He entered the large grocery store and I waited for him to emerge. He was in the shop for quite a long time and I wondered what could be keeping him. As I got out of my car and approached the shop I met a neighbour who had just left there and i asked her if she had seen him in the shop[. She laughed and said, 'Yes, he is in there and he is being a real nuisance. He is demanding to see the manager and asking who is the MP for this area as he claims his change is five pounds short and he's very persistent.' I entered the shop and watched him from a point where he could not see me. Sure enough this well-mannered, polite man was demanding in an angry tone, 'What are you going to do about it?' and he was rhyming off things that were wrong with the premises, his from tone commanding obedience. The young manageress was politely explaining that he would have to call in the following day as she could not do a till check until then. He had sobered up considerably, and I somehow realised he was enjoying his

insistent demands. Old habits die hard, I thought, as my mind went back to the incident Jeannie had described with the cigarette machine in the Barrowland Ballroom. The scene was the same now as it had been then.

The time was inevitably drawing near when I would have to bring the subject of the 'Bible John' murders into our conversations. My approach was helped by the coincidental appearance of an article in the *Daily Express* in early February 1993 on the unsolved murders. A brief outline on the case also mentioned that the Granada Television series *In Suspicious Circumstances* was to screen a half-hour documentary on the 'Bible John' murders on 23 March 1993 at 9 p.m. The next day I mentioned to John X that the programme was to be screened in six weeks time. He indicated interest and then changed the subject but I could see that he was slightly agitated by the information.

Six weeks passed without further reference to the murders, of the programme. I knew that he did not have television but I had a feeling he would turn up to see it. Sure enough, on the night it was to be screened, he called at my door about 7 p.m. I had gone out for 20 minutes on an errand and my wife spoke to him through our door post intercom system. I had told he never to open the door to him if I was out. When I got back my wife told me he had called. She said his speech was slurred and that she could see through the glass in the door that he was unsteady on his feet. 'He will be back,' I told her, but my wife disagreed, saying that he had had too much to drink and she thought his return would be unlikely. 'Wait and see,' I said. At 8.55 p.m. the doorbell rang and there he was – he had sobered up. My wife was amazed. He watched the programme intently and when it ended he said, 'I had a coat in 1969 identical to the one worn by the actor playing the part of "Bible John".' He went on to

say, 'The programme was lacking in detail, and did not reveal many clues.'

'Three months after the murder of Helen Puttock I was interviewed about it by the police,' he continued. I asked him why and he said, 'A few weeks before the murder I had fallen out with my parent, and was living in a bedsit in Clouston Street near Queen Margaret Drive in the West End of the city. The police had been tracing men who had lived in Earl Street up to the time of the murder. I had lived with my parents in Earl Street where the murder had taken place.

'It was a Sunday afternoon whey they arrived,' he recalled, 'and I was reading my Bible. In fact, when I invited them in my Bible was lying open on the table. They asked me if I could recall where I was on the night of the murder, and I told them I was at a meeting in the church I attended in Montague Street. One of the officers offered me a cigarette but I told him that I did not smoke.'

I had seen Paterson smoking, and in an earlier conversation he had told me, 'When I went to the dancing I always bought 20 cigarettes. I would smoke a few of them in a nearby pub before going into the dance hall.' I had offered him cigarettes on occasions and he had smoked them. In his pious moods he never smoked but when he had a drink I noticed he would buy a packet. He only smoked on occasions and would go without for weeks. I reminded him of his previous statement about buying cigarettes before going into the dance hall. His reply was not immediate; I could see he was flustered and thinking about the challenge. He was shaken and looked at me in confusion, and stuttered, 'I had given them up then.' The observation had got to him and he excused himself and left.

Two weeks had gone by and he had not visited so I called on him. I was wondering if he would still be friendly towards

me after his last visit. When he invited me in I noticed that he was not as talkative as usual and he seemed to be guarded in what he said. By talking in an unconcerned tone I could see him gradually relax and he was soon engrossed in conversation again. As he talked I studied the surroundings. On his sideboard was a photograph of a couple taken in the 1940s or 1950s. I asked him who they were and he said, 'That's mother and father.' There were other photographs which I took to be members of his family.

'Have you any photographs of yourself when you were young?' I asked him.

'No, I lost them when I moved here,' he replied.

'What about a photograph when you were in the Royal Air Force?' I asked in casual interest.

'No, I lost all the photographs of myself when I moved here,' he repeated.

How odd, I thought. The only photographs he has lost as the ones of himself.

Looking at the photograph of his parents * noted his mother was about five feet five inches tall with short brown hair. She had the height, hair and appearance of the three murder victims. There was a black wooden plaque with gold lettering on the far wall. I had not noticed t on my first visit as I had had my back to it then. It was a biblical quotation: 'He shall look after those that I have committed unto Him'. A shiver ran down my spine at the possible meaning of it. On several occasions over the many months during my scrutiny of him, he had shown a penchant for singing hymns. His favourite hymn, which he would sing frequently, was the old Salvationist hymn 'Power in the Blood' that he said his grandmother taught him.

It was now over a year and a half since I had first met John X. He displayed hypochondria among his

characteristics, and on many occasions he complained about his upper abdomen, even although his doctor could find no evidence of disease. The hypochondria and other traits which came to the fore could make his company trying. However, playing on his weaknesses and showing sympathy followed by a question enabled me to catch him off guard.

At times I would take a step back and have a good look at what I was trying to establish and with each appraisal I felt there were grounds to continue. 'what is your favourite book in the Bible?' I asked him.

'Revelations,' he replied.

'What about the Book of Numbers?' I asked.

'Oh, you are talking about murder,' he said.

One evening he had been telling me about his experiences in the Royal Air Force. I asked him if he had ever lived anywhere other than Glasgow since he had left the Air Force. 'I have always lived in Glasgow,' he said, 'but I quite like Dundee. i went there in 1979 and 1980.'

'What took you there, a holiday?' I asked.

'It was a change or venue,' he replied.

'Did you know someone there?' I continued.

'No, I did not know anyone,.' he answered. 'I stayed in a bed and breakfast both times, which were weekend stays.'

He had certainly proved to be a Pandora's box and i was sure this 'venue' would provide another surprise.

The time had come to take the bull by the horns and put it straight to him. His piety irritated me; he was expounding the Bible again when I interrupted his rhetoric. I spelled it out for him: 'I don't just think you are "Bible John" – I know you are.' I studied his reaction; he stared at the floor without speaking. I could see the consternation on his face.

After a few minutes he straightened up in his seat and said very quietly, 'I have to congratulate you. there were many

police officers searching for "Bible John" at the time, you are very clever!'

The atmosphere was electric and I was ready for anything. With his hands together as if in prayer, his fingers touching his lips, he sat in silence staring straight ahead in thought. After a few minutes he spoke again. I could see he was uneasy. I expected him to deny or even laugh off the suggestion, but he reverted to his familiar escape by changing the subject.

The following afternoon a neighbour who often sunned himself on the low wall opposite my home told me he had seen John X at ten o'clock that morning peering into my garden, obviously looking for me. My neighbour asked him, 'Are you looking for Donald?' My neighbour then told him I was out. Paterson replied, 'No, I am no looking for Donald, I am going to the library.' The same neighbour saw him again leaning over the garden gate about midday and he asked John X again if he was looking for me, and Paterson's reply once more was, 'No, I am going to the library.' At 3 p.m. he was seen again peering into the garden and when asked the same question by my neighbour he made the same excuse. The neighbour told me he was angered by this denial as Paterson was obviously looking for me.

At seven o'clock that night I was sweeping the driveway when he appeared. He looked strained and stood by the garage door as i swept. Then quietly he enquired, 'About the conversation we had last night, have you mentioned it to anyone else?'

'No, why should I?' I replied. 'If I went to the police and told them I had found "Bible John" they would probably lock me up.' You could see his obvious relief at my reply. When I had finished sweeping, we sat in the garage and I mentioned that a neighbour had seen him looking for me

three times that day. He denied it and said he had only passed once on his way to the library. I believe my other neighbour rather than John X. He was lying.

He suddenly asked if I knew if Helen Puttock had any brothers.

'I don't know, why do you ask?'

'If your accusation of last night got around. her brothers might come looking for me.'

He was more concerned with his own safety than with the accusations I had made about him. 'What do you think would happen to "Bible John" now, if he were caught?' he asked.

'I'm sure that the time lapse and the age of "Bible John" would be considered. whoever he is, he must have suffered over the years hiding his terrible secret,' I said. Tears were flowing down his cheeks and he covered his face with his hands and sobbed quietly. When he had composed himself, I continued. 'More than likely it was jealousy or hatred for a woman that had caused him to murder.'

He said, 'Maybe it was two women,' with a hint of knowing. 'By the way,' he added, 'the trail has gone cold. I have personally buried "Bible John".'

'The trail may have gone cold as there is no forensic evidence, but old habits die hard,' I told him.

For the next three days he called on me early and was hanging about all day. That in itself was strange, as he previously only called in the evening. Paterson needed to be near me. It was suspicious because a person with a direct connection to the murders would rather have distanced himself. He let slip that he was watching me. 'I saw you leaving in your car earlier from my window and yesterday I saw two men with clipboards going into your house.' He was right, as I had arranged for a surveyor to call. He was

sweating.

On the fourth day he called again early. It was his pay day, the day he did not usually visit. He had been drinking and I told him I was going out. He even suggested that he could go with me but I told him to go home. When I returned home early in the afternoon he was back again. He told me he had seen me arrive and thought he would call again. I reiterated that I was busy and that he should go home as he had had too much to drink.

The doorbell rang at 6.30 p.m.; he was back again. I was just sitting down to my tea and I was annoyed by his third interruption that day. When I opened the door he appeared to have sobered up. He said he had a very serious problem. 'What is it?' I asked.

'I have taken an overdose because i feel suicidal,' he said.
'What have you taken?' I asked.
'Thirty paracetemol,' he replied.

I told him to go home and i would call an ambulance. five minutes later I went to his home and sure enough the empty paracetemol packet was lying on his table. He had divided the tablets in two to make them easier to swallow. The ambulance and the police arrived. It was routine for the police to call in an attempted suicide. He was taken to the Western Infirmary.

The following day I was sitting in the garden when he walked through the gate smiling. This man never ceased to surprise. 'They kept me in overnight for observation after pumping my stomach. They wanted me to go to the Gartnavel Psychiatric Hospital but I told hem I was all right and signed myself out,' he said. I was relieved to see him as the attempted suicide had shaken me. I even worried that I had pushed him too far. I did not want to be responsible for his demise and I never mentioned the subject of "Bible

John" to him again.

Without prompting, he went on to tell me that he had tried to commit suicide before. 'On that occasion, I threw myself into the River Kelvin. When I hit the cold water I decided it was not such a good idea and I called for help; fortunately, two men arrived and pulled me out.'

'But why did you do it?' I asked.

'When my parents died I felt euphoric and for a couple of years after they died I was still euphoric, then I felt terribly low. That is why I did it.' I did not question his explanation, as I guessed that his euphoria had a hidden reason.

For the next three weeks he clung to me and his visits were frequent. I had the feeling that he had signed himself out of the hospital to be near me because he was worried that i would go to the police. At the end of the third week we were sitting in the garage having a dram. I was wary that he might try something but I was not afraid of him and he knew it. It was a warm summer evening and he was not talkative. He had had a few drams and his responses to me were grunts and growls, full of malice.

Sitting in an old armchair, with the garage light on as it had become dark, I had dosed off when I was awakened by a vice-like grip around my neck. His legs astride me and the full weight of his body behind him, he was strangling me so that I could not breathe. I gripped both his wrists and slowly forced his hands away from my throat and with all my strength stood up and pinned his arms above him against the garage wall. I was younger and fitter than him and his strength ebbed. I was angry and could see the hate in his face.

'What did you do that for?' I demanded.

He replied, 'I don't know why I did it, it just came over me. Maybe I have said too much, I should have cut your

throat,' he said and left. He did not come back for quite some time.

For the next eight months he went on a drunken spree. It was amazing that he did not kill himself as almost every day he was blind drunk. At the end of the eight months he had spent his entire savings of three-and-a-half thousand pounds on drink. I saw him a few times but he was furtive and kept to the back alleys when he went out, avoiding all contact. He was used to being a loner. I enquired about him through his next door neighbour who told me he was disturbing everyone in the close with his behaviour. She said he was signing hymns loudly at two and three in the morning and banging his table with his fist and shouting 'God is here'. 'It has been going on for months,' she said.

Three or four times I saw him in the dark deserted street about two in the morning, standing outside my house, staring up at the lounge window. He would stay for about fifteen minutes before slipping off. it was eerie. It had taken tow years getting to know him but I was sure there was more.

POWER IN THE BLOOD

CHAPTER 3

Numbers

And they shall be unto you cities for refuge from the avenger; that the manslayer die not, until He stand before the congregation in judgement.
(NUMBERS, CHAPTER 35, VERSE 12)

Three young women of a similar age had all been murdered within an eighteen-month period. Patricia Docker on 22 February 1968, Jemima McDonald on 16 August 1969 and Helen Puttock on 30 October 1969. they had met their killer in the Barrowland Ballroom. Patricia and Helen chose Thursday night while Jemima's visit was on a Saturday night.

Although Jeannie Williams, sister of Helen Puttock, had provided many details about her sister's killing, very little was known about the murder of Jemima McDonald and nothing at all about the murder of Patricia Docker. A pattern began to emerge when I noticed all the murders had taken place on even numbered dates. The months were even numbers as were the days of the week. This was the sequence: the twenty-second of the second month on the fourth day of the week; the sixteenth of the eighth month on the sixth day of the week; the thirtieth of the tenth month on the fourth day of the week. Linked to this was the pattern of the first murder in the south of the city, the second in the east

and the third in the west.

The killer had quoted the Bible and there had been much speculation as to which book in the Bible he had been quoting from. The police had never managed to pinpoint the biblical reference. Were the even numbers and points of the compass a serial killer's cryptic clues? Jeannie Williams had recognised that 'Bible John' had been quoting from the Old Testament. As there was a pattern to the numbers, could his quotes have come from the Book of Numbers? The Book deals with jealousy, adultery, iniquity, Moses and children, the unclean and the laws of murder. 'Bible John' had told Jeannie in the taxi that he disapproved of married women going to dance halls and considered them adulterous! All three women had been menstruating when they were murdered; presumably 'Bible John' regarded them as unclean!

In the Book of Numbers, chapter 35, verse 11, referring to the laws of murder, instructs the slayer to flee (Then ye shall appoint you cities to be cities of refuge for you: that the slayer may flee thither which killeth any person at unawares). A few days after the first murder Paterson had given up his job at Rolls-Royce and had gone to work as an unpaid lay preacher with the Pentecostal Church in the north-east of Scotland. Was he fleeing to a place of refuge? Was he interpreting the Book of Numbers literally as a licence to kill? The three young women had been killed by a religious madman who, in his warped mind, regarded them as unclean and adulterous.

When I asked Paterson in my discussions with him to name his favourite book in the Bible he mentioned the Book of Numbers, he had immediately said. 'Oh, you are talking about murder.'

Nothing at all had been known about the murder of

Patricia Docker, the first victim. The killer had to gain her confidence; so how did he do it? Patricia's husband was a corporal in the Royal Air Force and John X, the man I suspect is 'Bible John', had been a corporal in the Pay Corps of the Royal Air Force. Was it possible that he had won her over by his detailed knowledge of the Air Force together with his religious quotes? He told me that in 1968, although he had no licence, he bought and drove a white Ford Consul for six months then sold it to his brother-in-law. Three cars had been seen in the murder area on the night of the first murder: a Morris Traveller, a foreign car and a white Ford Consul, all of which were traced and eliminated from the enquiry. could there have been two white Ford Consuls in the area that night?

The murder of Jemima McDonald can be linked to that of Patricia Docker on several points. Jemima had been to the Barrowland Ballroom and two witnesses had described her partner as being 25 to 35 years of age, about six feet tall, of slim build, with short reddish fair hair, wearing a good suit and white shirt. She had been sitting in a pub near the dance hall with the suspect, and later they had been seen sitting together on a settee in the dance hall itself.

Jemima had been strangled with her own tights and her handbag was missing from the scene of the murder. She may have been murdered because, as previously mentioned, she had been menstruating at the time and may have rejected sexual advances. In the murderer's mind she was unclean and adulterous and had to be killed.

Helen Puttock, the third victim, and her sister Jeannie Williams, rode in a taxi with 'Bible John'. It is in Jeannie Williams's detailed story that the facts and individual clues merge! Her description of 'Bible John' and everything that he said can be linked to John X. She describes him as about

five feet ten inches in height, with short, sandy almost red hair. He was dressed in a well-cut brown suit mad of Reid and Taylor cloth, a blue shirt and a dark-blue tie with red stripes across it, similar to a military or old school tie. Paterson had described to me his can tie as dark blue with red stripes, bearing his clan crest.

As I have already revealed in Chapter Two, startling coincidences arose in my conversations with Paterson when compared to the conversation which took place in the taxi with Jeannie Williams on the night of her sister's murder. Remarkably, the conversations were almost word for word but coincidences will not stand up as evidence in court.

Stranger still is the incident when 'Bible John' produced a card or identification paper of some sort before leaving the dance hall and showed it to Helen. Jeannie was unable to see what this was but Helen's attitude changed from playful disbelief to surprised acceptance of him. Could it be that her reaction was due to the fact that this card or paper showed that they both lived in the same street, which was Earl Street?

However, around that time he had fallen out with his parents in Earl Street and was living in a bed-sit in Clouston Street. It is interesting to note that when the latter two murders had been committed, within two and a half months of each other, Paterson was staying in Clouston Street.

Paterson had a love-hate relationship with his mother which, together with whatever had caused the fall-out with his parents, could have triggered his murderous tendencies. The three victims had an uncanny resemblance to his mother. As Dr Robert P. Brittain described in *The Sadistic Murderer*: 'He is particularly likely to offend at a time when he has suffered a loss of self-esteem of if he feels that some event has challenged or denied his masculinity. The sadist who has

been laughed at by a woman, or mocked by his acquaintances, particularly in a sexual context, or who has been demoted or discharged from his employment, is likely to be at his most dangerous.'

When passing Kingsway in the taxi, 'Bible John' mentioned that his father had worked in that area at one time. An orphanage had once stood there, which led the police on a false trail thinking that 'Bible John' himself might have been a foster child. However, on the opposite side of the road was Albion Motors where Paterson's father had worked. Jeannie was surprised to hear him say something about foster homes or foster children and something about Moses and a woman who had been stoned, possibly a veiled allusion to the children of his previous two victims, and what was to come. He would have known about the orphanage that once stood at Kingsway as he had been brought up in the area and maybe that prompted the cryptic reference to children. At this point in the conversation the taxi was passing Albion Motors on the left and the site of the orphanage on the right.

'Bible John' told Jeannie he knew the pubs in Yoker. John X had talked to me of having a pint in a Yoker pub after work when he worked at Rolls-Royce in Hillington. Once when discussing work he told me that at school he had been very keen on science, especially when he got to use pipettes, and would have loved to work in a laboratory. 'Bible John' told Jeannie in the taxi that he worked in a laboratory, making special mention of the use of pipettes. The taxi driver who had taken the three passengers to their destination was unable to help the police. He was new to the job and had heard nothing of the conversation in the back of his cab that night.

After 'Bible John' had killed Helen Puttock he had been

seen boarding a night service bus at about 2 a.m. in a dishevelled state. Byres Road would have been his most direct route to Clouston Street but even at that time of night there would have been people about and it was well lit so, knowing the area well, he decided to alight at Gray Street where he would most probably have taken the following route, considering it the safest and best option. He would probably have gone via the dark, tree-lined Kelvin Way which leads onto Bank Street; then by crossing straight over Great Western Road and turning into Hamilton Park Avenue, then left into Hamilton Drive and right into Queen Margaret Drive, he would only have a short walk to the sanctuary of his flat in Clouston Street. He would have known that these quiet, shadowy streets would get him to his destination without being seen. In 1969 Paterson had worked as an insurance agent, his round covering the whole escape route, giving his detailed knowledge of the area and, as Jeannie had heard 'Bible John' say, he also knew the exact time of the buses and blue trains north of the city.

'Bible John's' height had been described as five foot ten inches. It is possible that his suede boots were of a type that enhanced his height by means of a hidden built-up inner heel. There were available by mail order in the sixties. Boots like these could have increased Paterson's height by about two-and-a-half inches so that if he was five feet eight inches tall, he could have increased his height to five feet ten-and-a-half inches. As has often happened in other cases, witnesses got his height wrong. He normally wore glasses and had a moustache, but by removing the glasses and shaving off the moustache, he was transformed into the divine messenger of death, 'Bible John'. As he was living away from his locality hardly anyone would have noticed this transformation of the stranger who had lived in Clouston

Street for a few months. He would go to ground for a few weeks and revert to his normal appearance of moustache and glasses.

When Paterson was interviewed a few months later by the murder hunt police, he told them that on the night of the murder he had been at a church meeting on the corner of Woodlands Road and Park Road. It is unlikely that this meeting in a church would have gone on beyond ten o'clock that night. I established through Paterson himself that the meeting in the church had indeed ended at 9.30 p.m., giving him plenty of time to shave off his moustache, lay off his glasses and head for the Barrowland Ballroom. John X was eliminated from the enquiry on the grounds of height, appearance and a slim alibi. Did his respectable veneer mask a callous killer?

Ex-Superintendent Joe Beattie thinks it probable that a policeman actually interviewed 'Bible John' in the early days without realising it. A lead probably emerged during a house-to-house enquiry; a lead which was neither recognised nor followed up on, giving the killer time to cover his tracks.

Could this interview by the murder hunt officers at Clouston Street have been the crucial lead that was not recognised or followed up? 'Bible John' was adept at going to ground and Joe Beattie is also convinced that someone harboured him in the early months of the murder hunt at the height of the hue and cry; and, after all, 'Bible John' was the typical 'mammy's boy'.

'Bible John' had deliberately set out to kill and had planned each murder carefully. The name John was obviously an assumed name. In my conversations with Paterson I established that his cousin and his brother-in-law were both called John. Certainly, he could have chosen the name at random, but the fact that the name was ready at hand

could have made it the obvious choice.

I tried many times to steer our conversations round to the subject of teeth and dentists but he always evaded any question about the name of his dentist. I never established if his natural front teeth overlapped. Was this one of the reasons he had 'lost' all photographs of himself when he was younger?

The murder squad made a search of all the tailors in Glasgow in the hope that a tailor somewhere might recognise a customer or the suit that 'Bible John' wore, and make a connection between the two. Paterson's clothes were purchased through his mother's account in Goldbergs so it is unlikely that the murder squad would have thought of checking purchases made in a woman's name. They were also ordered to check all hospitals. Paterson had been in Crichton Royal Psychiatric Hospital in Dumfries but this hospital was never checked by the police. Had they included it in their search they would have discovered that it admitted patients from the Glasgow area and it could have led them to the suspect.

Let us move on to the question of 'Did he kill again?'. After the killings of the sixties, there was a gap until about 1977 when there commenced another series of unsolved murders of young women in Scotland. Studying each new case in turn, it looks increasingly likely that having gone to ground for a period of about eight years, 'Bible John' had indeed resumed his deadly crusade.

The first of the 1977 murders is that of 20-year-old Anna Kenny from Gorbals in Glasgow. After a night out on 5 August in the company of a girlfriend, she left the Hurdy Gurdy bar in Lister Street, Townhead, to look for a taxi. It was believed she had been given a lift, but nothing at all was heard of her until her body was found by a shepherd almost

two years later on 24 April 1979 at Skipness in Kintyre. Her grave is known as Rockfield. A spade had been used to bury her body. Nothing more is known of the circumstances surrounding Anna's death and no one has been charged with her murder. The only thing which could link 'Bible John' to this murder is that it could have been a chance killing.

A chilling comparison can be drawn to the murder of Hilda McAuley, also in 1977, Hilda was 36 years old, lived in Drumlaken Street in the Maryhill district of Glasgow, and was the mother of two sons but had been divorced from their father in 1969.Her one night out was on a Saturday and on 1 October 1977 she went to the Plaza dance hall with her friends, leaving her children with their grandmother.

As usual she went for a drink beforehand to McNee's bar next to the Plaza where she was seen in the company of a man described as 30 to 35 years old, five feet eight inches tall and of slim build. He had neck-length dark hair brushed to one side and had a sallow complexion. She was also seen inside the dance hall just after midnight.

The following morning, 2 October, her battered body was found by several boys picking brambles in a lovers' lane at Westferry caravan site near Langbank in Renfrewshire. Her body was almost naked and items of clothing were scattered in the bushes. She had been strangled. Murder hunt detectives were looking for the driver of a van which had been parked without lights between 4 a.m. and 6 a.m. near the scene of the murder. The driver was traced and eliminated from the enquiry.

Enquiries again drew a complete blank but Detective Superintendent Douglas Meldrum adopted a similar line of enquiry to that used in the 'Bible John' murder investigations eight years earlier by Superintendent Joe Beattie. Three female detectives were sent to the Plaza dance hall in

plainclothes and although the police were certain Hilda had met her killer at the dance hall, they got no results.

Equally as horrific, but in the east of Scotland, are the murders of Christine Eadie and Helen Scott, two 17-year-olds whose bodies were found in East Lothian only two weeks later, on 16 October 1977. They were last seen alive the previous evening leaving the World's End pub in Edinburgh High Street. Police think the two girls were in the company of two men with whom they got into a car. Both were strangled and beaten, with their hands tied behind their backs. Despite extensive enquiries by the police in the Edinburgh area, this case also drew a blank.

Two months later, back in the Glasgow area, the body of Agnes Cooney was found at Snipe Road, Caldercruix, Lanarkshire, on 4 December 1977. When found by farmer John Stewart, the body had obviously lain there for some hours as her boots were covered in frost. There were bloodstains nearby, indicating that she had been killed at that spot.

She was last seen at the Clada Club just after midnight on Friday, 2 December, and left on her own. It was believed she had been held in captivity for about 24 hours before being driven out to Caldercruix and murdered. She was wearing a thin gold band on her wedding finger. When she had been identified, Detective Superintendent Gold and Chief Inspector Cowie set up murder headquarters at Craigie Street Police Office in Glasgow.

They established that she had gone with her friend Gina Barclay to the Clada Club which was near Glasgow's Plaza dance hall where Hilda McAuley had met her killer. Despite appeals for information from the public, this case also drew a blank. one man did call a national newspaper claiming to know the identity of the killer. When prompted to reveal this

he said, 'I am having a terrible time wrestling with my conscience,' and rang off. There are no other clues as to the identity of the killer and the case remains unsolved.

Yet another young woman from Glasgow was found murdered on 20 November 1978. Mary Gallagher, a 17-year-old from Springburn, was found near Barnhill Station in Springburn. She had left home the previous Sunday night to meet her friends, although she was never to meet them since she was waylaid by a killer. As in the other murders, the case remains unsolved.

Are these unsolved murders the work of 'Bible John'? Although there is an eight-year gap between the 'Bible John' murders in 1968–69 and the murders in the late seventies, these can be linked once again by the penchant for killing on even dates and even numbered months. The different *modus operandi* in two of the cases does not necessarily eliminate him as a suspect nor does it deny this man's drive to kill.

It was in the late seventies when my suspect began beating his father and callously attempted to have both parents committed to an asylum. Had they harboured their son for eight years knowing that he had a lust for killing? Under the threat of exposure, Paterson would have had much to fear from his parents. Perhaps this kept him under control for eight years? As his parents became more frail with age they may have lost their control over him. Paterson made a strange remark when his parents died. 'I felt euphoric when my parents died and for a couple of years after they died I was still euphoric.' Was this euphoria because they had died taking the secret of their son's murderous tendencies to the grave?

Let us consider again the findings of Gerard Croiset the clairvoyant, brought in by the police to assist in the enquiry into the murder of Helen Puttock. Mr Croiset's expertise had

been proved many times before. He mentioned an old man who knew something about the murders, indicating that the murderer lived in the south-west of the city, and described 'Bible John's' personality and characteristics. On a map of Glasgow he sketched an area on the south side of the River Clyde towards Govan where he claimed both the old man and 'Bible John' lived, predicting that a large engine would be found in the area, near a scrapyard. Croiset correctly guessed that the area was in the west of Glasgow but wrongly stated that it was on the south side of the river. My suspect and his father lived on the north side of the river. The gigantic crane known as 'Goliath', at one time used to lift steam trains on to ships for export, could be the large engine to which Croiset was referring. Goliath was on the north of the river, and to the west of it were several scrapyards containing old cars, off South Street. Croiset had described them as just off a main road. The scrapyards extended as far as Earl Street. Both South Street and Earl Street run parallel with Dumbarton Road – the main road.

The points of the compass are mentioned at the beginning of this chapter. In the Book of Numbers, chapter two, verse two, it instructs the tribes of Israel how to arrange themselves in camps: *Far off about the tabernacle of the congregation shall they pitch*. It goes on to instruct: *Go to the south, the east, the west and the north and set your standards*. In Chapter Two of this book, Paterson described how he visited all the churches throughout Glasgow, in the south, east, west and north of the city. There is a similar pattern in the murders; the first murder in the south, the second in the east, the third in the west. As if to compensate for the eight years since the murders in the late sixties, among the new series of murders recorded in the late seventies were one or two connected to the north of the city.

It is as if the distinct pattern established by the serial killer had been disrupted, both by the visit from the police in Clouston Street and by the control exerted over him by his parents who knew he was 'Bible John'. My suspect believed he was a divine messenger and, as such, was compelled to complete his pattern of the compass points. It is interesting to note that they form the shape of the cross when completed. Are these cryptic clues of a serial killer which have not been noticed?

Paterson can be placed in the Edinburgh area at the time of the killings of the two 17-year-old girls, Christine Eadie and Helen Scott, and also that of Agnes Cooney. He was employed as a timekeeper clerk by a construction company at North Queensferry, where he stayed in lodgings during the week and spent the weekends in Glasgow. His duties included checking vehicle fuel consumption and the distribution of vehicles and ignition keys to drivers. Although Paterson had no licence he was able to dive, so this duty provided the opportunity to borrow vehicles at random which would have facilitated his weekend jaunts to Glasgow or Edinburgh.

In the murder of Agnes Cooney it is interesting to note that Caldercruix, where her body was found, is situated on the Old Edinburgh road, the A89, which runs parallel on the north side of the M8. Its route from Glasgow to Bathgate leads onto the Forth Road Bridge and North Queensferry. It was thought that the killer had either driven from Glasgow and back again after killing Agnes or that he lived in the area of the killings. Agnes could have been kept trussed, or beaten unconscious in the vehicle during he 24-hour captivity, then driven to Caldercruix in the early hours of the morning whereupon she may have been dragged from the vehicle and then murdered.

If my suspect was responsible for Agnes Cooney's murder it is possible that he planned it along these lines – certainly he had the opportunity and the means and by leaving no traces of blood in the borrowed vehicle and returning it to the contractor's site at North Queensferry before the other workers arrived on the Monday morning, it would be virtually impossible to link it to the events of the weekend. Paterson himself, whether at work or in his lodgings in North Queensferry, would be many miles from the scene of the murder and almost certain to avoid suspicion, since the murder hunt would almost likely be concentrate in Caldercruix sand Glasgow. the thin gold ring Agnes was wearing on her wedding finger and which had belonged to her mother might well have sealed her fate as she would have been regarded as married and adulterous. Patricia Docker had been wearing a wedding ring when she was murdered in 1968. Those who weren't wearing a wedding ring probably told the killer they were married or separated and it sealed their fate, and he murdered those who weren't married believing they were. The first three victims in the late 1960s had all been menstruating. It is now clear that it was sheer coincidence; if they were married then that was the reason they were killed.

And so the catalogue of killings of young women who had spent the last day of their lives dancing in the happy, exciting atmosphere of Glasgow dance venues, ended. By the late seventies the Barrowland Ballroom, the Majestic Ballroom and the Albert Ballroom had long since closed their doors with the advent of the new-style nightclub discotheques. Only the Plaza Ballroom remained open with its old-style dance bands catering for the dancers who, over four decades, had preferred the formal atmosphere to the informal, deafening music of the discotheques coming into

vogue at that time.

Keep in mind that the murders in the late seventies occurred in and around the old-fashioned Plaza Ballroom. 'Bible John', when he first struck in the late sixties, was described as being about 34 years old, so at the time of the later murders he would have been in his early forties. The combination of his age and the decline of the old-style dance halls, he knew,m would eventually narrow down the number of suspects and potentially lead to his capture if he continued his crusade of murder in his home town. Glasgow was getting too hot for him and it was time to seek new venues.

Let us consider again Paterson's remark about his two visits to Dundee in 1979 and 1980. He did not refer to them as holidays or weekends away but said, strangely, 'It was a change of venue'. I decided to make enquiries of my own into any unsolved murders of young women in Dundee, especially those who had been dancing. This provided startling results. I had outlined the details of my enquiries to a reporter with a Dundee newspaper. I asked her to provide me with information concerning unsolved murders of young women between 1970 and 1984, particularly those carried out in the 'Bible John' style.

A few days later she forwarded the information I had been seeing. She found that there were several unsolved murders, but only two fitted the required category. The victims were Carol Lannen and Elizabeth McCabe. Their murders in Dundee in 1979 and 1980 respectively have become arguably the most baffling crimes to take place in the city, and remain unsolved to this day. Their deaths are technically separate cases but they are known as one – the Lannen-McCabe murders.

On the afternoon of 21 March a young couple out walking in the Templeton Woods made the grim discovery of Carol's

naked body partially covered with snow. She was 18 years old and the mother of a three-month-old child. Templeton Woods are on the north-west outskirts of the city, some 150 yards from Templeton Road. Carol had lived with her sister in Hill Street, had last been seen alive shortly before eight o'clock the previous night getting into a red Cortina-type estate care in Exchange Street, near Commercial Street – an area then accepted as the city's red-light district.

On 1 April some of Carol's clothing and personal effects were found on the banks of the River Don near Kintore about 12 miles from Aberdeen.

A red estate-type car was seen on the bridge over the Don at Kintore on 22 and 23 March.

Tayside Police issued a photofit picture of a man they were seeking in connection with the Carol Lannen murder hunt. This photofit was assembled from descriptions given by witnesses who saw the driver of the red Cortina-type estate car whi h Carol was seen entering in Exchange street on 20 March 1979.

The man was described as of thin build, pale complexion, short, dark hair and short sideburns. He was well spoken and clean shaven apart from a moustached which covered the upper lip and looked as though it needed trimming.

Less than a year later, as the first anniversary of Carol's killing approached, Templeton Woods were yet again to yield a grim discovery.

In the early afternoon of 26 February, sadly the day before what would have been her 21st birthday, the body of nursery nurse Elizabeth McCabe was found deep within an area of small fir trees in Templeton Woods.

Her body lay just 150 yards from where Carol Lannen had been found. Elizabeth McCabe had been strangled, the same method used to kill Carol Lannen. Elizabeth's naked body

had been discovered by two youths walking their dogs and her clothing and handbag were later located in three different parts of the city.

The petite 20-year-old was last seen alive at Teazers discotheque in Union Street in Dundee at about 12.30 a.m. on Monday, 11 February, when she told friends she was going home.

The discovery of Elizabeth's body was a tragic end to the long days of waiting for news of their daughter by parents James and Ann McCabe.

The eldest of their family of three daughters and a son, Elizabeth was last seen alive by her parents on 10 February when she left the family home to meet a girlfriend for a night out in the centre of the city. One theory suggested is that she got into a car thinking it was a taxi.

So, did Carol and Elizabeth meet their deaths at the hands of the same killer? There are similarities in both cases – the age of the victims, the fact they were both picked up in the centre of the city and that the handbags of both women had been removed from the scene and, perhaps the most striking, they were found only 150 yards apart, with clothing removed. Thousands of people the length and breadth of Britain were interviewed as part of the investigations into the Lannen-McCabe murders. Sadly both trails went cold but it does appear to me that the similarities are so remarkable as to conclusively point to one killer – 'Bible John'.

The first murder in Glasgow in 1968 of Patricia Docker has the same features as these latest murders in Dundee; the removal of clothes, the missing handbags and the penchant for killing or setting out to kill on even dates.

Were these two murders in Dundee 'Bible John's' final killings? His definite signature, his style, is plain to see.

The murderer of Hilda McAuley in 1977 was described as

having dark hair. Did the possibly greying-haired 'Bible John' of the late seventies dye his hair when he committed the later murders in Glasgow and Dundee?

The resemblance between the photofit picture of the Dundee killer and that of 'Bible John' is striking. When dark hair and a dark moustache are superimposed onto the 'Bible John' photofit the results are startlingly alike.

I am not saying that 'Bible John' committed all of these murders but what I am suggesting is that they are all worthy of consideration – some more than others. The murder of Patricia Docker on 22 February 1968 had heralded the beginning of the 'Bible John' murders and the murder of Elizabeth McCabe in Dundee on 10 February 1980 marking the end. Was the killer using even greater cunning by committing his murders further afield? Was this what Paterson meant when he said he had gone to Dundee 'fir a change of venue'? This seemingly introspective man displays a pretence of Christian conformity which does not correspond with his behaviour and his outward demeanour belies a belligerent, impetuous hatred towards females. He is indifferent to others and his murderous frustration easily triggered by the mere mention of adulterous and unclean women. This behaviour has remained mostly unaltered by experience. He has a perverse misogyny. In psychiatric terms he would be diagnosed as having a sociopathic personality . . . 'a serial killer'. The pattern of the serial killer is -lain to see. His signature of even numbered dates, even numbered months and even numbered years from the first murder to the last is obvious – from February 1968 to February 1980.

Dundee may have marked the end of the killings but the story is not yet finished.

CHAPTER 4

Judges

Ye shall not respect person in judgement; but ye shall hear the small as well as the great; ye shall not be afraid of the face of man; for the judgement is God's; and the cause that is too hard for you, Bring it unto me, and I will hear it.
(DEUTERONOMY, CHAPTER 1, VERSE 17)

Paterson had been on a drinking spree for several months and I felt concern for his well-being. After I had put it to him that he was 'Bible John' I did a lot of soul-searching for I feared that he could overdose again and I would have felt responsible.

I called to see him, taking a neighbour along with me. He took a long time to respond to our knocking on his door and when he eventually opened it he was clearly in a terrible state. He was shaking uncontrollably due to his heavy drinking but he managed to relate with difficulty, in a confused and garbled conversation, that he had taken too many of his prescribed anti-depressants and tranquillisers, which compounded his condition.

He was trembling so much that when I poured him a glass of milk from a bottle in the kitchen and held it for him to drink, his teeth chattered against the glass and the contents, which he had difficulty in swallowing, spilled down his front. I felt a terrible pang of guilt and was extremely sorry

for him as I had probably contributed to his state. I asked him if I should call his doctor but he indicated that he did not want his doctor involved.

I sat with him for a while, but found any conversation difficult as his speech was so slurred. I supposed it was a silly question but I asked him what had got him into such a state. He managed to blurt out clearly, 'It is something I did in the past . . . a long time ago, and I am having a terrible time wrestling with my conscience.' My thoughts went back immediately to the murder of Agnes Cooney when a mysterious caller to a national newspaper used the same sentence, word for word. My feeling of guilt evaporated. It was difficult to ignore the possibility that this man was 'Bible John', as each time I was in Paterson's company he seemed unwittingly to let slip a confession.

I was aware that innocent people in the past had been drawn into high-profile murder investigations and I had a strong feeling that this was happening to me, incredibly on this occasion not by the police, but by the perpetrator.

Four days later I met him in the street, now fully recovered, and I invited him round to my home for a chat that evening. I had hidden a tape recorder before he arrived at 7 p.m. I was determined to capture him on tape so I had to get him talking freely by leading him on to key questions without making it too obvious. I opened the conversation with general chit-chat and then steered it round to the subject of smoking, pointing out that if I were to give up smoking I would be able to save enough money to buy golf clubs and take up that sport. I reminded him that he h himself in the past had played golf. Surprisingly he talked openly. I also reminded him that he had told me on a previous occasion that he had smoked Embassy tipped cigarettes but during my taping he deliberately avoided naming the brand, merely

saying it was a tipped cigarette.

Getting him on tape was important, as much of what he said coincided with the clues that were known to the police. He continually used 'mother and father' to describe his parents; he mentioned that his granny had been a Salvationist and that he had two sisters. ('Bible John' had talked to Jeannie in the taxi about a sister and Jeannie recounted later how he was about to say something further when he stopped what he was saying mid-sentence as if he suddenly realised he was revealing too much. Was he about to mention a second sister when discretion stopped him?)

Paterson went on to say on the tape that some people are naturally perceptive. At that point I asked him if he thought I had been perceptive in his case. He replied, 'I don't know – it remains to be seen just how we go from now on.' He had lowered his voice as he uttered this statement and there was a hint of a challenge in his tone.

He went on to relate how his parents has thrown him out of the house for four days in 1972. I asked him, 'Why?'

'Oh, it is just things you do under the influence of drink,' he replied.

'What did you do?' I pressed.

'It is just that you do things under drink that you wouldn't do normally; I gave my mother a fright.'

'What did you do to give your mother a fright?' I asked.

'It does not matter,' he replied. 'I just gave her a fright – and my father as well. My behaviour was a bit wild but there we are, that is in the past . . . I am glad, I am glad,' he added in a suddenly most pitiful voice.

As if to justify his actions he went on to relate, 'I once mentioned to an elder in the church that I had tried to kill my father and the elder told me he once picked up his father (he's a big chap this elder I'm speaking about); he said he

picked his father up when he was drunk and threw him across the room.'

'But why did you try to kill your father? Was he annoying you?' I asked.

'No, I don't know why. It was just the same as that bloke when he was drunk who picked up his father and threw him across the room, and his father was a Christian.'

'What did you do to try and kill your father; did you punch or try to strangle him or did you try to hit him with a hammer?'

'Well, I've told you before I tried to strangle him.'

'What happened – did you get away with it? I remember you told me that the police came to see you.'

'Not on that occasion. The poor man was just lying there and I just put him to bed.'

'Was your mother there?'

'No, she was in hospital at the time.'

'Did you strangle him unconscious?'

'No . . . no, no, I just, eh, the rope just came round and it unloosened itself.'

'A rope?'

'The rope which I had tied round his neck. I put a slip knot on it to strangle him and when I pulled it, it unloosened. It was a miracle actually; it shouldn't have come loose.'

'Otherwise you would have killed your father?'

'Possibly, possibly.'

'So you put a slip knot on it?'

'Yes." And you would have actually taken his life?'

'That's right, that was the last . . . that was the last time, eh, the first time . . . the first, the rope when I pulled and the tension of tightening that rope and eh, instead of it tightening it just unloosed itself, now it shouldn't have done so.'

'but what sort of slip knot did you put in it?'

'Just a knot that would slip. You know what a slip knot is?'

'You must have put it on quickly, the slip knot?'

'No, no, I just put it on. And it just slipped off.'

'Otherwise he would have been dead?'

'I mean exactly what I am telling you. Don't try to explain it all. I mean I'm telling you it was a slip knot and it should have been tightened but it didn't.'

'But what prompted you to do that? He must have been pestering you?'

'No, he wasn't, he wasn't!'

'But what the hell did he do?'

'He wasn't doing anything, I was drunk and this had just happened, just happened.'

This taped conversation I played over and over again. What was most chilling was the casual way he spoke about strangling his father. It seemed curious to me that he would use a rope. I recall his mentioning that when he was a lad he was in the Sea Scouts and had learned to tie different knots, which he said fascinated him even now. This fascination with knots didn't explain the use of a rope within a domestic situation. Somewhere in the back of my mind I recalled reading that certain killers have an obsession with tying knots. I decided to store the subject for consideration later.

Other bizarre happenings would transpire over the next few weeks, causing me to sever any further contact with Paterson.

The first of these happenings occurred a week later. I had met him in the street and invited him to a local bar. The time passed amiably and we headed home in the early evening. When we parted company he seemed in good cheer but what I was to learn a few days later from Paterson himself was, to say the least, disturbing. He had gone straight home, opened

a window and, lying down on the floor, had called for help. Two passers-by in the street heard his cries and went to his aid. He told them he was having difficulty moving his limbs. He was a bit vague about what happened next but it appears the police came on the scene and he had told them he had suffered a sudden paralysis and he believed that I had poisoned him. I confirmed a few days later that the incident had indeed taken place. The second incident took place a week later when he called at my home at 10 p.m. and it was obvious that he had had a drink. I told him I was about to settle down and watch an interesting programme on television. He joined me but was continually disruptive in a deliberate manner throughout the programme and after several such interruptions, I told him that if he didn't behave he would have to leave. His response was one of malicious defiance and so he was thrown out. Fifteen minutes later the police called at my home to inform me that Paterson had complained that I had tried to kidnap him. The police officer obviously saw the funny side of it and left. I wonder what he would have thought if i had counterclaimed that i suspected that the accuser in this instance was none other than 'Bible John'.

A seemingly strange set of incidents took place several weeks later. It started with Paterson arriving at my gate in a black Hackney cab. At first I ignored this as it was a public road after all and there wasn't much I could do about it. Over a period of three weeks it happened on six occasions. When the taxi pulled up, Paterson, after paying his fare, would walk towards my fate and open it but when the taxi disappeared round the corner he would close the gate and stare up at my house before moving off in the direction of his own home. What was he up to? He seemed to be trying to give the taxi driver the impression that my house was in fact

where he lived and it took my mind back to one of the things Jeannie Williams had reported as having been said during that fateful taxi journey which ultimately led to his sister's murder. 'Bible John' had told he he had plenty of money! Paterson was obviously trying to create that kind of impression.

Then round about that same time a most revealing incident took place in my garage. A local shopkeeper whom I knew quite well had been having a spate of break-ins to his shop. He asked if he could watch from my garage, as it was possible to observe his shop through a small gap in the garage door when it was closed. I agreed to allow him to do this and so we arranged to meet and keep a watch between midnight and two in the morning when the break-ins were happening. At about 12.15 a.m. we heard a taxi stop outside my house and I stepped outside into the darkness. As the taxi drew away, I heard the latch on the garden gate click and a figure stepped in momentarily while he waited for the taxi to disappear. It was Paterson and just as he was closing the gate to leave, I stepped forward out of the darkness and asked what he was doing. He stammered the excuse that he had thought he could see a light on in the house and he was going to ring the bell but had changed his mind. I knew this wasn't true as I had watched this odd behaviour with taxis over several weeks. My curiosity in Paterson was so strong that I was always keen to talk to him on any pretext and, given what I had gleaned from him to date, any opportunity to observe him further was welcome.

I deliberately showed no sign of annoyance at this intrusion and invited him into the garage for a dram. We went inside closing the door behind us and although the garage light was off, the street lamp outside shed enough light through the clear perspex roof so that we could see one

another reasonably well. Paterson must have expected me to be alone and at first he didn't notice the shopkeeper sitting in the semi-darkness and he showed signs of surprise when he discovered I had company. We explained our purpose and I poured him a drink; it was obvious he had already been drinking. The shopkeeper and I resumed our conversation as to whether his shop would be raided that night. Paterson remained quiet and sullen, demonstrating an uncalled-for aloofness if the shopkeeper spoke to him. I had observed this trait in him on previous occasions in the garage with other visitors. It was as if he was jealous sin some way, wanting to be the sole focus of my attention. I had gained his trust and it seemed as though he didn't want others to get too close to him. Jeannie Williams had described the same trait in 'Bible John'.

His attitude towards the shopkeeper became aggressive and the latter looked over to me in surprise. Paterson had been with us no more than 15 minutes and he was being malicious. I warned him about his attitude but he continued to bait the shopkeeper with venomous verbal abuse. There were two sides to Paterson – holy and sanctimonious on the one hand, the malicious devil on the other. He displayed the latter that night. I had observed on previous occasions in the past that he could be very polite but it was just superficial and that's as far as it went; beneath the front he didn't really have the true 'milk of human kindness'.

The shopkeeper, a Sikh, was becoming angrier by the minute as Paterson persisted in his verbal abuse. I realised that his remarks were becoming racist and more challenging and in a flash they were grappling with each other. The shopkeeper had punched him and I leapt between them in an attempt to diffused the situation, managing to calm the shopkeeper who was extremely angry by then and swore that

he would kill him. I jokingly replied, 'Don't do that, he might be "Bible John"! I don't want him dead.'

Paterson suddenly broke down crying. 'Yes, it was me, it was me. I was "Bible John". Oh, my God, it was me!' He was sobbing uncontrollably, the tears running down his cheeks and he cupped his face in his hands and continued to sob and mutter through his hands, 'Oh, my God, it was me. Yes, yes. I was "Bible John".' In the semi-darkness I looked at the shopkeeper who was contemplating this scene with an uncomprehending amazement.

All his aggression spent, Paterson's pent-up emotions seemed to have surfaced. He was still crying bitterly when I suggested to him it would be better if he went home and I saw him out to the street whereupon he walked away, sobbing, in the direction of his house. I don't think I've ever seen a man cry so bitterly as he did that night; I was stunned.

The curtains of his flat remained drawn for many weeks; he had gone to ground. Once or twice, as I glanced up at his windows from my garden, I saw his curtains move slightly and although there were no sightings of him, I knew he was there.

It was time to act on the information I had compiled over three years. The first person I confided in was a young CID officer who was investigating a theft from a neighbour's car. He had called to ask me if I had seen or heard anything the night before in relation to the theft and he listened to me with interest as I gave him a brief outline of my suspicions. When he left he promised to look into what I had disclosed to him. Six weeks later I met the same officer in the street outside my home just as he was about to get into his car and I asked him if he had followed up what I'd told him. He assured me that he had tried and went on to say that Paterson was the most elusive man that he had ever tried to speak to and that

he had been unable to make contact with him ever after repeated calls to his home, finally coming to the conclusion that he was away on holiday. I assured him that he was not on holiday and he was most certainly around. 'The only time he goes out is on a Wednesday; he is simply not answering when you call.'

I never heard the outcome from the CID officer.

Shortly afterwards the Glasgow *Evening Times* ran a three-day article on the 'Bible John' killings, with an invitation in the third and final article to anyone with information to contact the newspaper. I contacted the newspaper office and spoke to their crime correspondent and outlined my story. He arranged to call at my home the next day for a detailed chat. He arrived at the appointed time and for a few hours I was able to relate my story to him in fuller detail. After listening intently he acknowledged that I had made many interesting points. Then when I played the taped recording of my conversation with Paterson he asked me for a copy of the tape to allow him to listen to it more closely and we agreed to meet a few days later.

After a couple of days, as arranged, he telephoned and asked me to go along to the *Evening Times* office for a further chat. When I arrived he asked me to clear up some points that he'd not been sure of. That done, I asked him what he thought of the whole story.

He told me that for the past 23 years he'd had a suspect of his own but since hearing my story, my suspect was now also his new suspect. As for the tape recording, he went on, 'In my many years as a crime correspondent, I have heard of many instruments and methods used in domestic violence: kicking, punching, stabbing, axes, shooting, you name it, but never have I heard of a rope being used.' He asked if I had a photograph of my suspect as he had a plan. It so happened

that I did have one which I had taken of Paterson in my garden.

Then he told me he intended to visit Jeannie Williams, the sister of Bible John's' third victim, Helen Puttock. 'I want to play this tape to her and show her the recent photograph to see if she recognises anything relevant in the taped conversation or in the photograph. The following day the reporter set off for the quiet Ayrshire town to which Jeannie had moved a number of years ago. It was agreed that he should speak to her alone and that I should remain in the car. He emphasised that everything about my story could hang on Jeannie's opinion of the tape and the photograph. He was gone for about an hour and on his return he related Jeannie's opinion.

On hearing the tape recording she had said that the well-spoken voice was similar to that of 'Bible John' but that it was slightly deeper. However, she conceded that ageing could account for the deeper voice. The repeated use of 'No, no' by Paterson on the tape definitely reminded her of that specific speech pattern favoured by 'Bible John'. He had peppered his conversation with this double 'No, no', she distinctly recalled. As for the recent photograph of Paterson; she indicated that the hair was the same style, the eyes were the same and the nose was the same but that the mouth and cheeks could be sunken due to ageing.

Obviously, the reporter had deemed the story worthy of consideration, since z week later I was visited by two senior officers from the Serious Crime Squad who called at my home to hear my version of events which they noted carefully. They spent more than an hour doing so and on leaving told me they would inform me of the outcome in a few weeks. Six weeks later one of them telephoned me to tell me that they had eliminated Paterson from their enquiries on

the grounds that he did not conform to the height of five feet ten inches. He was an inch and a half too short. Witnesses at the time of the 'Bible John' murders described his height as five feet ten to six feet.

I was neither disappointed nor confused at this outcome but I decided to leave it alone for a while and gather my thoughts. I knew there had been many coincidences and circumstances leading up to that point and I knew there was the possibility that I had been wrong about Paterson. Call it what you will; intuition, luck, good fortune, sixth sense, insight, they are all one and the same and I determined not to let it go. But what course could I take after this seemingly final outcome? I recalled the case of the London railway rapist and murderer who had spread fear in the suburbs of London by stalking, raping and killing several young women in the early to mid 1980s. He was John Francis Duffy who was jailed for life for the murders in 1987. Before he was caught, seven witnesses, each one resent at the railway station location of a different murder, had independently provided the police with the description of a man seen hanging about at the time. All gave a similar description of his appearance and height which they believed was bout five feet seven inches. When this man was caught, all the descriptions had been accurate except for his height – which was five feet three! If those witnesses got it wrong so too could the witnesses in the 'Bible John' murders.

Shortly after the *Evening Times* article, a woman who did not want to be name contacted and met the same reporter and told the story of her narrow escape from a man who, she said, was definitely 'Bible John'. This occurred in February 1970 and she said she didn't go to the police at the time as she had been very afraid and although it was a long time ago she was still worried that her name or address might be

published, such was her fear. She told how she had gone to the Albert Ballroom where she met the man who at first meeting was very charming. She had several dances with him and when the band played the last dance he asked to escort her home. She agreed and they set off walking towards London Road and beyond towards Bridgeton, in the east of the city, where she lived at the time. She told him she had two young children but was separated from her husband. Their route passed quite close to MacKeith Street where Jemima McDonald had been murdered and the man, who by that time was causing her to feel increasingly uneasy, pointed out MacKeith Street and the tenement where the murder had taken place. As they continued on towards her home, which was a ten-minute walk from MacKeith Street, he suddenly told her he disapproved of married women going to the dancing and talked of adulterous women and the Bible. By then she was feeling more and more alarmed by the stranger, and he suddenly clamped his hand over her mouth and dragged her into the close-mouth of a derelict building and proceeded to try to strangle her. She recalled her terror as his hands tightened in a crushing vice as she fought to try and stay conscious while his fingers cut off her air supply. Then from the street outside she could hear the click of stiletto heels approaching and this, she believes, is what saved her life. The stranger eased the pressure on her throat as the footsteps came closer and she managed with great effort to break away and run into the street towards the couple whose footsteps she had heard. The stranger followed her into the street but hesitated when she reached the couple. At that moment a taxi neared them and the stranger stepped out in the road holding his hand up to hail it. The taxi stopped and after the stranger had climbed in, it turned around and headed back towards the city centre.

The woman described him as being well spoken, with reddish, fair hair, of slim build, about five feet eight to five feet nine, smartly dressed, and he had been wearing a camel hair coat. This rekindled my interest in Paterson as i recalled his remark after watching the 'Bible John' programme on television.

'I had a coat like that then,' he had said, referring to the coat the actor in the television programme had been wearing. It was a camel hair coat. In fact, i remembered a conversation I had had with Paterson on a previous occasion but I hadn't seen the significance of that conversation at the time. He had been wearing a camel hair coat and I had remarked that it was a good coat. Paterson had gone on to tell me that over the years he had always worn a camel hair coat.

'As soon as one coat was worn out I replaced it with another similar new one,' he said.

But the subject of the coat takes on a more sinister implication. If we go back to Jeannie Williams's account of events on the night of her sister's murder, a few points should be considered again. First of all, there is her description of the way 'Bible John' straightened his scarf before putting on his coat as they prepared to leave the dance hall. Then there is the time-scale of the ensuring events and the way the sequence of these events was carefully calculated by 'Bible John', who began by making sure that Jeannie was dropped off first, leaving him alone with Helen. The taxi journey to Jeannie's drop-off point had taken about 20 minutes, with probably a further ten minutes' drive to where Helen lived. So, if they set off from Barrowland at about midnight, thy would have finally arrived in Earl Street around 12.30 a.m.

I would assumed that, having decided to kill his victim,

'Bible John' would certainly not have risked being in her company in that area for long., for fear of being seen and possibly identified, so he would probably have enticed Helen to the back-court and killed her quickly. It would have been all over in about 15 minutes at the most. So, where was he for the next hour and a quarter untill he boarded the bus at 2.00 a.m.? It was a good 20 minutes walk from the point where he killed Helen to where he boarded the bus but that would still have left him with near enough an hour to spare and any stranger to the area, after committing murder, would want to be well clear of the scene rapidly. More to the point – where was the coat he had been wearing? The witness on the bus said he had mud on his jacket.. There is no mention of a coat! Had he ditched it? Where was it? In his murderous struggle with Helen it must have got muddied and stained.

If 'Bible John' and my suspect Paterson are one and the same, the following scenario could provide a believable explanation. Paterson's parents lived in Earl Street. Could this be where the murderer had taken refuge for an hour, discarding his coat there? Then, with his knowledge of public transport, he was fully aware that he could easily catch that late-night bus. He was cunning! Jeannie and other witnesses would describe him wearing a coat when last seen, whereas he knew that as a coatless man it might help cover his trail. Anyway, he had to get clear of Earl Street and his parents' house as he knew there would be door-to-door enquiries the following day and a reddish, fair-haired man with a scratch on his face would have been hauled in immediately for questioning and identified by Helen Puttock's sister Jeannie. He may well have slipped into his parents' home without their knowledge, leaving again in plenty of time to walk to the point where he boarded the bus and was transported away from the scene of the crime,

alighting at Gray Street, whereupon he made his way to his room in Clouston Street.

It would be several months before he was interviewed there giving him long enough to compose himself and dispose of evidence such as the clothes and the suede boots he had been wearing. If his parents had covered for him, he had duped everyone an d succeeded in throwing the investigators off the scent.

Here were two women who had been in the company of 'Bible John' for at least two hours but in spite of this he had avoided detection. i decided on a new plan of action – a direct approach to ex-Detective Superintendent Joe Beattie.

* * *

The hunt for the killer of Helen Puttock must have been the most disappointing case in Detective Superintendent Joe Beattie's career. This was no slipshod investigation but the most thorough manhunt Scotland had ever seen. The atmosphere of hopelessness and frustration must have been almost palpable amongst the murder-hunt team. They had covered every avenue, exhausted every lead, and as the days grew into weeks and the weeks to months they were still no nearer to catching 'Bible John'. The net had been cast wide and Joe believes that 'Bible John' was in that net; and so do I. Joe was a very astute police officer and an excellent leader but in the end, any leader is only as good as his team; he cannot do everything himself, so inevitably we must come to the conclusion that one of the team let 'Bible John' slip through the net.

Then came the criticism and the suggestion from other senior officers that Joe was relying too much on the one witness, Jeannie Williams. Why the criticism? She was, after all, the most important witness. Who other than this sister of

the victim Helen Puttock could have recalled and described in detail the characteristics of the killer? Other witnesses had only seen him briefly and presumably the other John, Jeannie's dancing partner who never came forward – selfishly to protect his own skin – was a married man out on the town without his wife's knowledge.

Many critics had been judging the handling of the case, but no one knew better than Detective Superintendent Joe Beattie the implications of this. Not only did they fail to get their man, but the reputation of the Glasgow police was at stake. Even now, 26 years on, should these murders be solved and the others attributed to 'Bible John', there should be no comfort in hindsight for the critics. The murders rank alongside those of Victorian London's Jack the Ripper.

I was playing my last card. Officialdom had rejected my claims, so my approach to ex-Detective Superintendent Joe Beattie, with all that had gone before, was tentative. I contacted Joe by telephone and, apologising for my intrusion into hi private life, I briefly explained the reason for my call and asked if he would be interested in reading the rough draft of the circumstantial evidence I had gathered to date. He agreed to read it and I posted it off to him and awaited his response, if any. A week later Joe telephoned me to tell me it was certainly worthy of investigation. I then asked him if he'd be interested in listening to the taped conversation I'd had with Paterson. Again he agreed to listen to the tape, which I forwarded to him. Ten days later Joe telephoned me to tell me he thought the contents of the tape were extremely interesting. I informed him that Jeannie had heard the tape and I relayed to him her remarks about it and her opinion of the recent photograph of Paterson. Joe went on to say that he had checked and discovered that Paterson had indeed been interviewed at Clouston Street by one of his officers and that

he had not been among the many hundreds of men that he himself had interviewed. Now, given the background I had provided him with, he said Paterson should be been a prime suspect. He went on to say how flabbergasted he was that this man had not been drawn to his attention at the time of the murder hunt and that, if he had, he would have been the subject of closer scrutiny.

I told him of my meeting with the investigative journalist and the subsequent visit from the Serious Crime Squad and the outcome of that. He told me to leave it with him and, having noted my comments on this visitation, he added, 'I will go into this in more depth when we meet but suffice to say that they do not have the same interest in the subject that I do. It would appear,' he went on, 'that there is a lack of official interest and while I would not want to do anything which might prejudice any ultimate outcome, I think something should be done. Truthfully, I think the best thing would be to get Jeannie to see this bloke – I am certain that if it is he should would have no hesitation in saying "Yea" or "Nay".' Making contact with Mr Beattie was to be the start of lengthy correspondence and numerous telephone conversations about this mutual interest and has continued over two years up to the present day.

I was to discover many qualities about ex-Superintendent Joe Beattie that have to be admired. First and foremost is his tremendous sense of humour and his humanity. In his capacity as a police officer, a career that has spanned over 30 years, he was aware that the many criminals he had encountered were in some cases mad, in others downright bad and, as he put it, some were poor, sad souls. One of the qualities that made him a successful police officer was that he was approachable and the job had not made him cynical, as is often the case., He is a man who has lived with life-and-

death situations in the police, and as a fighter pilot in World War II. Although he has been retired for the past 20 years he has a razor-sharp mind for detail and recollection which is kept well honed to this day.

It was several months from my first contact with Joe before we actually met. For Joe, I'm sure it was a convenient, though unusual, meeting place. This tryst took place in the comfort of a ward in a Glasgow hospital where Joe had been undergoing treatment as a day-patient and it was there we came face to face. I'm sure that Joe had chosen these surroundings wisely, rather than his home ground. After all, he did not know me nor I him. Over the years he must have encountered theories on the 'Bible John' m murders from cranks. We did not broach the subject of our meeting immediately and I could sense that Joe was no fool and that you wouldn't easily pull the wool over the eyes of this sagacious man.

I was relaxed in his company as he talked casually about his treatment and the usual everyday concerns of life. It was towards the end of our meeting that we talked about and exchanged views on the case. As we parted company I am sure that Joe had gauged the sincerity of my convictions. It had been agreed that Joe would do what he could to expedite matters. He asked if it would be all right with me if he forwarded the rough draft and the tape recording, together with his opinion, to the Serious Crime Squad, to which I readily agreed.

Living in such close proximity to Paterson it was inevitable that we should meet from time to time and my interest was such that I could not distance myself and I maintained friendly conversation with him when we met in the street. On one such meeting with him he looked really shaken and he told me had had just had a bit of a fright,

going on to tell me that he had spotted a woman in the street whom he had not seen for over 20 years and that that was what had given him the fright. I was intrigued and prompted him to elaborate but he wouldn't be more specific. I was puzzled; why should he mention it if he was not prepared to explain the details? Instead he explained it away with his usual remark, 'It doesn't matter.' However, it mattered to me and I wondered if it could possibly have been Jeannie Williams whom he had seen. I contacted Joe and explained the situation, asking him to establish from Jeannie if she had been in Glasgow on the day in question. Joe got back to me and told me that he had spoken with her but she had not been in Glasgow that day. So, who was this woman who had given Paterson such a fright? Was it the woman whom he had tried to strangle and who had managed to escape his clutches? I contacted the investigative journalist about my suspicions, but in order to protect her anonymity, he would only confirm that she was now living in the West End within our proximity. Was it she? I never established who it was but given the track record, it was possible.

Several weeks later two senior officers from the Serious Crime Squad called at my home. I invited them in and when I asked them to sit down they declined. Their attitude was menacing and one of them slammed a large brown envelope containing the rough draft and my tape recording onto the coffee table and announced, 'Keep away from Joe Beattie. He is an old man and you are pestering him. We have already eliminated this suspect on his height both in 1969 and now.' They left as quickly as they had arrived before I could say anything. I was stunned.

It left me wondering what had transpired between them and Joe. It occurred to me that maybe Jo had been merely humouring me and had complained that I was being a

nuisance. This somehow didn't seem to fit as he had been definite in his interest. 'He may be an old man,' I thought, 'but he could teach them a thing or two.' I was angry. A few days later I telephoned Joe to apologise if I had indeed been a nuisance but he very soon explained what had happened. On the day that these two officers had called at his home, he was at the hospital for his day-care treatment and, in fact, he had not seen them at all. His wife had been at home alone and Joe explained that she had spoken to them expressing her concern about her husband's involvement in the case now that he was retired and that she believed it was contributing to his ill-health. This was a very understandable reaction. However, Joe assured me that he was determined to speak to these officers and put the points of the case to them, stressing that it had been an unforeseeable turn of events which had led to their attitude towards me.

A considerable time later they eventually, at his prompting, revisited Joe and he was able to put points to them regarding Paterson. He later told me that one of the officers, on the question of Paterson's height, had referred to him as being 'a wee shilpit cratur'! Joe quickly pointed out, 'I am too, if it comes down to it – but I have not always been like this and neither has he!'

Joe's efforts to spur officialdom on led to nothing, or at least they didn't divulge, nor were they obliged to divulge police business. I thought of many reasons for the police's disinclination to become involved again: the age of the case, the lack of forensic evidence, budget restrictions, a preoccupation with current cases, or else, somewhere along the line someone had put the plug on the I was a nutter feeding Joe's obsession with the case. I put it to Joe that I thought it would be a simple matter to obtain a photograph of Paterson in his RAF days for Jeannie to have a look at and

also to let her see this man in person. Joe agreed that he would have followed these lines if he were still a serving officer but, unfortunately, as things stood, he couldn't really intervene.

At about this time Joe received a telephone call from a doctor friend of his from whom he had heard nothing since about the time of Helen Puttock's murder. Joe was surprised to hear from his friend after so many years and even more surprised when he went on to apologise for the lengthy time gap, telling Joe that he had always meant to contact him about a patient of his who had had difficulty in relating to women. He said that this man had lived in Earl Street in Scotstoun, had red hair, was also a Bible thumper and had lived with his elderly parents. Joe told me of this and I immediately asked if it was the same name as my suspect, to which he replied that it wasn't.

Was it possible that there had been two red-headed Bible thumpers staying with their parents in the same street, both with severe problems relating to women? I had the feeling that either the doctor had not wanted to betray his patient's confidence while revealing this information to Joe, or that Joe hadn't wanted to betray his friend's confidence when he had told me the story, leaving me to put two and two together myself that they were one and the same. Otherwise both of these men had evaded the dragnet in the murder hunt. I concluded that it was just one man – Paterson. Truth is truly stranger than fiction.

Months passed and Joe and I conceded that we were banging our heads against a brick wall. It was back to square one. The only course of action left, I told Joe, was to go public and that I was going to write a book. 'And what a book it would make,' Joe replied. I must admit, however, that Joe never committed himself at any time by saying that

he thought my suspect was 'Bible John', though he did tell me once that when he was a serving police officer he would classify a case as 'cold, warm or hot'. When I asked him about this case he did say that he thought it was 'hot'.

This is the story up to this point as it unfolded but it is far from over as there are still more surprises to come. I was determined to persevere. 'Evil flourishes when good men do nothing about it.' I had been judging John X solely on his own revelations. My observations of his behaviour led me to another objective way of looking at the whole situation.

POWER IN THE BLOOD

CHAPTER 5

Chronicles

Therefore thus sayeth the Lord God; because ye have made your iniquity to be remembered, in that your transgressions are discovered, so that in all your doings your sins do appear; because I say, that ye are come to remembrance, ye shall be taken with the hand.
(EZEKIEL, CHAPTER 21, VERSE 24)

On occasions forensic psychiatrists and suchlike experts have helped the police by drawing up psychological profiles describing the type of person they should be looking for when a major crime had been committed. In this instance, at the request of the police, the forensic psychiatrist Dr Robert P. Brittain had drawn up a profile specifically to help in the hunt for 'Bible John'. I already knew that the police used psychological profiling to help in detection and so I went back over all the facts that I had compiled – facts which in themselves were startling enough – reviewing them now in conjunction with Brittain's profile. I discovered that this profile fitted the personality and actions that I had observed in my suspect up until that time; not only that, but some most stunning incidents which happened later also fitted the pattern, indicating the possibility that John X was the killer and that the urge to kill was still there. Brittain wrote:

The forensic psychiatrist is sometimes asked by the police whether he can describe the type of person they should be looking for when a major crime has been committed. What can be done in this field remains limited and this must be said clearly at the outset. The question frequently arises in cases of murder and in particular the sexual murder. It seemed therefore of value to attempt to draw such a profile in the specific case of sadistic murderers. The more precise the description which can be given, the more probable becomes their early detection and the greater hope there is of eventually being able to recognise them before they have killed. It is useless, though it is sometimes done, simply to label such a person a psychopath and then give a textbook description of psychopathy. This is not only too broad to be of value to the police, for example, but it is also not accurate. It is also important to distinguish the murderer who kills in a sexual setting, as for example the killing of a taunting, unsatisfied sexual partner or killing to silence a victim of rape, from the true sadistic murderer who alone is considered in this paper, although these can be factors in his case also.

The picture that is drawn below is derived from over 20 years of experience in forensic pathology and forensic psychiatry, from observing scenes of crime, from the examination of victims and, above all, from the examination and continued study of sexual murderers themselves rather than from psychiatric theory. It has been drawn, deliberately, without returning to examine the literature. Inevitably knowledge of the literature will be reflected in it although it will not always be in agreement with what has been written. Deliberately, no attempt has been made to quantify the data used nor to explain in detail the features mentioned. The purpose is to try to give a factual description for practical

use, not a theoretical formulation.

Before trying to describe what such a murderer will be like it is perhaps well to give the warning, unnecessary to the experienced, that there should be no unfounded preconceptions. Such a preconception might be to think of him as a large, hulking brute, of low intelligence, with overt and easily recognisable elements of aggression, outgoing, loud, insensitive, rough, crude, vulgar, oversexed and a known sensualist, with a history of mental illness and a record of major aggressive sexual offences. some sadistic sexual offenders have certain of these elements but the majority may appear to be much like other people.

It is also true that no one should be ruled out as a suspect because of preconceptions, whatever they may be, for the acts of such a murderer reflect the deviations of his mind and these he conceals as best he can from others, and even close relatives may have little idea of his abnormalities.

It is, however, possible to list the characteristics commonly found in sadistic murderers and this can be a guide. It is a surprising and, at times, even a bizarre picture. If it is known, evidence which might otherwise have been overlooked can be sought and given its proper value.

The picture drawn below is a composite one and thus not every such murderer will fit it and none will show all the characteristics mentioned. Most, however, will match the description to some degree, and some very closely.

The sadistic murderer is almost always male. Female sadistic murderers are rare and will not be considered in the description that follows.

He is commonly introspective and rather withdrawn. He has few associates and usually no close friends. His pursuits are solitary, for example, in his spare time he reads or listens to music alone or goes to the cinema by himself (often to see

horror films), rather than play football in a team or go drinking in a group. He may appear as studious, pedantic, retiring, shy and even as an inadequate personality, with a lack of drive. Sometimes he presents as a-pseudo-intellectual. He is described by those who know him as quiet, reserved, uncommunicative, withdrawn, well mannered, mild natured, agreeable and, not infrequently, as being timid and never showing temper. He does not retaliate to violence and never did, even at school. In view of this it can be hard to believe that he could be capable of extreme, sexually motivated violence and he is thus easily discounted as a suspect. He can often become embarrassed, even in ordinary social situations, and blushes readily. Obsessional traits may be observed and evidence of these may sometimes be noted even at the scene of the crime. For example, the victim's shoes may have been carefully and neatly placed side by side, perhaps in a setting of general disorder. He may be known to be a particularly tidy person, sometimes meticulous in dress and appearance and very clean.

He feels different from others and thus is different and isolated, knowing that he cannot relate well with them, and so is insecure.

Not uncommonly he neither drinks nor smokes and alcohol probably plays a much smaller part in murders my such persons than in most other categories of homicide. Sometimes he has experimented with drugs though he is not, in my experience, addicted to them.

He may feel himself to be an inferior being except as regards his offences. The planning or contemplation of these acts can make him feel superior to other men, someone special or even godlike. Others then become to him inferior creatures, without rights, to be used in any way he wishes

for his gratification.

He is particularly likely to offend at a time when he has suffered a loss of self-esteem of if he feels that some event has challenged or denied his masculinity. The sadist who has been laughed at by a woman or mocked by his acquaintances, particularly in a sexual context, or who has been demoted or discharged from his employment is likely to be at his most dangerous.

He can be prim, proper, even prudish, avoiding profanities himself and condemning obscenity, vulgarity or impropriety in others. He condemns sexual conversation and deplores 'blue' stories.

In many cases the sadistic murderer is a vain, narcissistic, egocentric individual who, through his vanity, may be convinced that he can commit murder and escape detection by being more clever than the police. He would rather be notorious than ignored and, although his life is a rather withdrawn one, he may have ideas of himself going down in history as a major criminal and, before detection, read and comment on details of his crime reported in the newspapers., He sometimes expresses very strong and punitive views on what should be done with the murderer when he is caught. There can be a peculiar arrogance about him.

He can be hypochondrial and is commonly apprehensive of even the most minor surgical procedure.

Beneath his retiring façade there is a deep aggression which he cannot normally express.

Sometimes, but by no means always, he is recognised by acquaintances as being 'strange', off-beat', 'twisted', a 'loner', 'kinky' or a 'weirdie'.

His manner may be considered effeminate but this may show simply as what might be called an over-politeness or over-refinement for his social group. It can sometimes be to

the degree that the suspicion of homosexuality may arise, though he does not usually present as being homosexual. Not infrequently he has a history (though not usually a conviction) of some homosexual activity, though this may have been of a minor nature and known only to the participants. Some may express a great aversion to homosexuals. In the case where the victim of sadistic murder is a boy or a man, the murderer may be more overtly homosexual.

He is typically a day-dreamer with a very rich, active fantasy life. He imagines sadistic scenes and these he acts out in his killings. He dwells on atrocities such as were committed by the Nazis and on others, more extreme still, of his own invention. The extremes of cruelty and the ingenuity he can show in this are almost inconceivable until one sees, for example, his drawings of his fantasies. Even as a child he is likely to have been withdrawn, living in part in his own dream world. His fantasy life is in many ways more important to him than his ordinary life, and in a sense more real, so diminishing the value he puts on external life and on other people. It is almost as if he were forced by practical realities to emerge unwillingly from fantasy at times but returns to it as soon as he can.

It seems possible that most sadists restrict themselves to fantasy and that only a minority act out their imaginings in criminal acts and ever come to notice. If this view is correct, it suggests a larger reservoir of potential offenders than is usually suspected.

There is no limitation by social group. He is generally under the age of 35 years. He is usually of high intelligence, which is probably necessary for a rich, complicated fantasy life. His high intelligence is also important in that it allows careful planning of the offence and assists in the avoidance

of detection.

Emotionally he is flattened for the cruelties he fantasises and for the crimes he commits. If he were not, he could not tolerate the thought of them. It is as if, by long exposing himself to his fantasies of extreme cruelty, he had become cynically and coldly indifferent to the tragic and the horrible, and entirely insensitive to cruelty inflicted by himself – though not necessarily by others. His is thus without remorse or conscience as regards his offences, no matter what the cruelty involved. He is not concerned with the moral implications of his acts and treats them casually. He is without pity for his victim. He will frequently express regret if asked, but he does not feel it, or, if he does, his feeling is only transiently sincere, is shallow and is quite insufficient to prevent him from killing again. Such expressions of regret are commonly to create what he hopes is the right impression and one designed to achieve some advantage for himself. He can detach himself from his killing, being aware of it but not emotionally involved. He knows that he is responsible for his offence but regrets only its legal consequences.

After his crime he will often behave normally, returning home to eat and sleep well. The fact that deep remorse does not cloud his thinking and his judgement can be a protection to him if he is suspect, and his calmness can make it more difficult for others to believe that he could be guilty. On questioning about the crime he does not become emotionally upset and agitated, as would be expected, but remains unperturbed. Intellectually he *knows* that it is wrong to kill but emotionally he does not *feel* this to apply in his case. He is indifferent to the feelings of others but shows much concern in matters relating to himself and in particular to his welfare or his safety.

Physically he may be small or of poor physique, but is by no means always so. He often considers himself to be under-endowed as regards his sexual organs even when these are normal, as they commonly, though not invariably, are. This feeling of sexual inferiority as compared with other men may partly explain why many such persons find it difficult to urinate or undress when other are present, and so earn themselves a reputation for excessive modesty.

He is often sexually weak with feeble potency and it is his concern about this which is of prime importance rather than the defective potency itself. In short, he is not virile in any sense. Usually he is unmarried, has shown little or no interest in girlfriends, and finds it difficult to make advances to women. He has a fear of adult contacts, both social and sexual, and some even have an active hatred of females. He may have had little or no experience of normal sexual intercourse.

The seeds of his abnormalities would seem to be planted at a very early age and a careful history will often show clear evidence of some manifestations of his perversions even before puberty.

Surprising as it may seem, his fantasies, interests and practices do not always make religion unacceptable to him, and sometimes there is not only a declared interest in it but he may be a church-attender. He can also be sanctimonious and sometimes quotes scripture. spiritualism seems to make a particular appeal to some of these men.

He may describe opposing forces warring within him, referring to them as good and evil, or God and the devil. He may talk of hearing two voices, one telling him to do wicked things, the other telling him not to. On close questioning these voices seem to be pseudo-hallucinations. Sometimes he talks of being possessed, 'something inside me, other

than myself, exerting an influence over me'.

Often there is no prior criminal history but sometimes there is and it is then commonly of a sexual offence. This may be of a non-violent character and without obvious relationship to sadistic murder – offences such as stealing female underclothing from clothes lines, Peeping Tom activities, obscene telephone calls, etc. (It does not follow that all who commit such acts are potentially sexual murderers and many may only be social nuisances; it does follow, however, that such offenders should be examined most carefully because a proportion, however small, are potentially very dangerous.) Some have a history of fire-raising.

Again commonly there is no personal and often no family history of mental illness. He does not normally seek psychiatric advice for he has no doubt as to his own sanity, does not always recognise the degree or significance of his abnormality, is probably afraid that he would meet with a lack of understanding or even condemnation and may fear also that his source of gratification would be taken from him by treatment without being replaced by an equally potent source of pleasure. If he has come to the notice of a psychiatrist at all it is probably as a result of a prior sexual offence such as those mentioned. He is mentally a very abnormal person, as will become even more clear as his characteristics are more fully outlined, but this abnormality will not necessarily be obvious at any ordinary interview and he may talk and behave in a perfectly ordinary fashion. If the characteristics of the group are known, and thus the proper questions asked, the position may be clarified.

It is the active fantasy life, the emotional flattening (though here it is a localised one) and the introversion, I think, which makes doctors sometimes wonder if such a

person is, or will become, schizophrenic. I have known one such case have a brief schizophrenic episode and two others each had a brother who was reported to have suffered from schizophrenia. Most sadistic murderers, I believe, are not schizophrenic and do not become so. Sometimes they talk of hearing voices, perhaps of a dead relative. There are not usually directly related to their offences and do not seem to be true hallucinations. They are not grossly psychotic and not insane within the McNaughton Rules, for they know the nature and quality of their acts and know that they are wrong. They would not commit murder, not only if there were a policeman standing by, but even if they thought at the time that there were any real possibility of their being caught. Occasionally, however, a case is seen which seems close to psychosis of a schizophrenic type but these appear to occur among those who show the general symptomatology of the syndrome but who have not acted out their fantasies in killing.

A person with the syndrome being described occasionally presents as a patient with an anxiety state and I have now also seen three who had depressive illnesses, but none of these has committed murder. It may be that the anxiety or depression is a result of resistance to murderous drives.

The work record of such men may be poor and their occupations may vary widely. Sometimes they show their inclinations by getting employment where their desire for power and control over people or animals can be expressed, or where they can act out their desire for violence, though their personalities can restrict the possibilities open to them. A surprising number have worked as butchers and if the choice of employment lay between that or being a slaughterhouse worker on the one hand, or an office worker

on the other, there is no doubt as to which they would prefer. An occasional one says he would like to be a dress designer, but these have only been among those who show the general symptomatology of the group and I have not yet seen this among those who have committed murder. A history of a suspect's prior occupations is thus worth eliciting. It would also be possible to suggest other occupations which might attract the potential sadistic murderer or, at least, which it would not be surprising if such a murderer had chosen.

Not infrequently there is an inordinate interest in weapons, guns, knives, etc., and he may have a large collection of them, but they have an attraction for him far beyond what they have for the ordinary collector and he may 'love' them, handling, and in the case of firearms, dismantling them and cleaning them for long periods at a time. He has strong feelings about them, may have special favourites and he can even have 'pet' names for these. Some carry a loaded weapon and explain that this gives them a feeling of pleasure, or safety, or power, and they can be unhappy without it. They can explain that with it they could keep people at a distance in a way that would be impossible with a knife.

Such a man has, frequently, a strong, ambivalent relationship to his mother, both loving her and hating her. He is often known as a particularly devoted son, emotionally very closely bound to her, bringing her gifts to a degree beyond the ordinary. He is a 'mother's boy' even when adult. There is also a deep hatred of her, not superficially obvious and not always acknowledged even to himself. He sometimes kills his mother and all male matricides should be examined with this psychopathology in mind. He often tells of having, as a child, seen his mother undressed.

The mothers are themselves interesting. They may seem

pleasant, very motherly, kindly persons, distressed by the murder their son has committed but remaining devoted to him. Later it is sometimes found that when they come to visit them they bring books and magazines and when these are examined they are found to deal with matters of a sadistic, criminal or pornographic nature.

In some cases the father is known to have been very authoritarian and punitive and may have, or have had, employment in civilian life or an appointment in the services consonant with this.

A grandmother, at least in Scotland, is occasionally an important figure to these men. Her death causes them acute distress and they may talk of hearing her voice or seeing her ghost shortly after her decease and they have even told of sitting for long periods beside her grave.

These men suffer not from a single sexual perversion but from a number of perversions. These often require privacy when they are being performed; so there may be knowledge that they lock themselves away in rooms for hours, or that they have a shed or other private place where no one else is allowed to enter. What some of these materials are will be mentioned as their commoner deviations are discussed.

Many dress up in female clothing at times. Such transvesting does not necessarily mean that they are homosexual. (This is another pitfall for the inexperienced because only about one transvestist in three is homosexual in his practices and some are married and may have children.) Unlike certain other transvestists, they do not usually wish to be seen by others when dressed as women and no one may know that they do this. When they start the practice they most commonly use clothing belonging to their mothers or sometimes to sisters. Later they may obtain it by theft from clothes lines or by ordering it by post from mail-

order businesses. Any kind of female clothing, outer wear or underwear, may be found, as may wigs, false breasts, sanitary towels, etc. There may be a large mirror in which they can watch themselves transvested, while they indulge in various sexual fantasies and they may even kiss their own reflection. One man who showed most of the features of the syndrome was an adult homosexual pederast. He admitted interfering sexually with small boys and had a desire to kill them, but had not done so. When asked if he transvested he denied it, but when asked if he had ever stolen clothing he said that he had – boys' clothing – and had dressed up in it.

They are sometimes known to be interested in photography and at least a few photograph themselves when transvested and some take pornographic photographs of others.

Their sadism is manifested in various ways. They are excited by cruelty whether in books or in films, in fact or in fantasy. There is sometimes a history of extreme cruelty to animals. Paradoxically they can also be very fond of animals. Such cruelty is particularly significant when it relates to cats, dogs, birds and farm animals, though it can also be directed towards lower forms of animal life, and the only animal which seems to be safe is one belonging to the sadist himself. Stabbing or hanging is perhaps the commonest expression of such cruelty, but it can go even far beyond this. There may be clear evidence of it in childhood, even before puberty.

For these men, cruelty may not be attractive except in relation to their perversions and they can be quite tender-hearted in other ways and vociferously condemn cruelty in others without apparently seeing any incongruity in this. To some at least, cruelty may not be so much the end they are seeking as the means whereby they arouse extreme sexual

emotion in themselves and it is the relief of sexual tensions which is their true aim.

Some are devotees of ;chambers of horrors' in waxworks and have paid many visits to such places.

A feature very frequently to be found in sadistic murderers is a consuming interest in Nazism and, in particular, in Nazi concentration camps. A number have fantasies of working in concentration camps and will describe the tortures they would use. They can express strong feelings and marked prejudices against coloured people. Some collect badges, daggers, uniforms or medals, particularly those related to Nazism, and may dress up in these. A less usual, but not rare, finding is an inordinate interest in, and even practise of, black magic. They may have stuck pins into photographs of people whom they wished to injure, or even have tried to invoke evil spirits. These interests in Nazism and black magic seem to arise because in both there is to be found the desired admixture of cruelty, sex and power over others. They feel Nazism ad black magic grant them personal authority to commit forbidden acts of extreme cruelty and absolve them from guilt and responsibility.

Another bizarre finding, also by no means rare, is an interest in monsters. These may be prehistoric monsters such as the dinosaur. They may be fictional ones of the King Kong type. They may be those of folklore, such as the werewolf or the vampire, and the man with this syndrome may say that he would like to be one of these. Finally, they may be purely imaginary, half-human, half-animal creatures, or horrific, twisted, perverted parodies of the human form, grotesque, horrible, ugly and evil. They may make drawings or models of these, or have pictures of them.

A few write poetry which reflects their abnormalities.

These people read, study and collect books which relate in some way to their perversion and it would be easy to give a list of those commonly found. Some are fiction, some are not. It is sufficient, however, to say that they commonly relate to some of the following: De Sade and his works, sadism, torture, cruelty, Nazism, Hitler, Goering, Eichmann and other Nazi leaders, concentration camps, prisoner-of-war camps, atrocities, brutalities, black magic, sexual perversions, obscenities, erotica generally – occidental and oriental, guns and other weapons, or uniforms. Less often there are books on war, crime and criminals, murders and murderers, psychology, psychiatry, forensic medicine, toxicology or 'escapology' or the tying of knots. As yet they do not seem to have discovered the writings of Machiavelli or Nietzsche (though Leopold, of the Leopold and Loeb case in America, is said to have been a student of Nietzsche's writings), but it would not be surprising if these were to be found in such a case.

There may be evidence of great interest in pornography, particularly heterosexual, sadistic pornography as found in certain magazines (mostly American in origin). For some of these there seems to be an almost unvarying formula, even for the coloured front covers which show soldiers in uniform, usually Germans; swastikas; a scene of violence; firearms; scantily clad young females in danger or distress; words such as sin, lust, sex, nude, death, virile, vice, Satan, devil, etc. The sadistic man may have made additions to the pictures, for example, manacles may be drawn on the wrists, Pornographic photographs may be found. Sometimes pornographic and sadistic scenes are drawn by the man himself, and very masculine women are not infrequently depicted. While such a drawing is of a woman, with a feminine hairstyle and wearing a skirt, part of her dress is

often a uniform, perhaps with a necktie, epaulettes, Same Browne belt, and sometimes with Nazi insignia. Scenes of violence may be drawn, and sometimes red ink or even blood may be used in such drawings.

Sadism and masochism are commonly associated and there may be evidence of masochistic practices. There may be ropes for self-tying or self-hanging, straps, chains or handcuffs (which may be mode-made). whips or other instruments of punishment or torture may also be present. Sometimes the murder victim is tied up with ropes.

Evidence of fetishism may also be shown. Rubber or plastic materials may be found or there can be pictures of fetishistic objects.

The murder itself may be carefully planned in advance and preparations made for it even days or weeks ahead. He may, for example, carry ligatures with him to use on an as yet unselected victim or he may follow his chosen victim over a considerable period. He can think it all out very clearly and wait until he finds a suitable time, place and subject and manipulate circumstances to achieve this. Such careful planning by an intelligent man, and where there is little to associated the victim with the murderer, the victim being selected by chance or for some reason not apparent to others, can make the murderer's detection particularly difficult. This difficulty can be enhanced by the fact that he is commonly a plausible liar and presents a front which can be mask-like, or one of injured innocence, and which is difficult to break. Even in the less common case where the sadistic murderer is of low intelligence, he can show a surprising degree of cunning.

At the time of the crime itself he becomes very excited and usually uses more force than is required merely to kill, though this is true of many other murderers also. He is now

transformed into a very different person from the shy, timid, withdrawn individual he so often appears to his acquaintances. His reason is dulled and his sexual drive and his desire for power take over control of his actions.

The sight of suffering can excite him further and his brutality can be increased by the helplessness and fear of his victim. During the act the ecstasy he experiences seems to make him frenzied and insensible to everything else, yet if something occurs which threatens his safety he can take appropriate action. Excitement seems to be greatest during the process of killing and the death itself may be an anti-climax.

The method of killing, except which gross and mutilating violence or multiple stabbing is used – the less common forms – is almost asphyxial, and a gag may occasionally be employed. This could be explained as being due to the positions of the murderer and his victim in a sexual attack being such as to make manual strangulation, or sometimes strangulation by a ligature, an easy and convenient way. It could also be explained as being associated with preventing the victim from crying out. There is no doubt that there is truth in both of these explanations but this is not the complete story. Such men will sometimes explain that shooting, for example, is too sudden a way of killing the victim, for their pleasure would be ended too quickly. They will explain that in asphyxia, by increasing or decreasing the pressure, they have it in their power to give their victims their lives or to take their lives from them. They can feel this as a godlike power, and they can play with their victims like a cat with a mouse.

This desire to have power over others is an essential part of their abnormality and if the victim resists they become the more determined and brutal. If the subjection of the victim

to their owners is more important to them than the infliction of pain, this may help us to understand why they do not feel cruel, for they may be aware that cruelty is not their primary objective but only the means whereby they achieve their end.

Other injuries, whether found in association with asphyxia or not, are most commonly on the breasts, on the genitalia, or in the rectum. If there is gross, mutilating violence it is likely to affect the abdomen also, or there may be the finding of very many stab wounds. Bite marks may be found and are most commonly on the breasts or neck of the victim but they are not restricted to these sites. They can vary from being minor to very severe. They can occur in homosexual as well as heterosexual sadistic murders.

Although these are essentially sexually motivated crimes, sexual intercourse or even orgasm does not always occur. Sometimes the murderer masturbates beside his victim. Sometimes also a phallus-substitute is used and a piece of wood, a cylindrical electric torch or other similar object, may be inserted _ and this can be with great force – into the vagina or rectum of the victim.

The victim is commonly found in the position in which the criminal assault took place, without any attempt, for example, to arrange the limbs but rather as if left in this way as a final degradation. It is as if there were a deliberate attempt to offend modesty.

After the crime has been completed the murderer may, as he describes, feel relaxed and experience a great relief of tension. Sometimes there is a feeling of disappointment as he may find he has not achieved the degree of pleasure, excitement and thrill which he had anticipated, nor yet a solution to his problems. therefore he can commit murder again in further attempts to gain relief of a tension which is

essentially sexual and recurring. If he does commit further crimes, as is likely if he is not apprehended, he tends to be reasonably faithful to the methods he has already used.

In court he can be self-possessed, calm and unperturbed, listening to he evidence of his actions with indifference and, indeed, something close to boredom.

It seems possible, the motivation and actions of such people being so little understood, in particular by those concerned in the legal proceedings, that the accused is often grateful that more of his abnormalities are not elicited in court and exposed to consideration. He may thus accept more readily and without question the evidence which is produced.

When he admits to his crime, or talks of it after being found guilty, any expression of regret for what he has done carries little conviction. A few will never talk of their crime at any time and may appear uninterested, contemptuous or evasive, but many will, and talk freely and fully and without embarrassment or feeling for their victims and often with bland unconcern. They can remember the circumstances and, if they will, can relate them clearly and with a wealth of detail. They often give an honest account and do not seem to be very suggestible.

Such men seem to enjoy talking of what they have done and to get satisfaction of an exhibitionistic kind from this and will often say they feel better after talking thus freely. A few will take pleasure in writing a detailed account of what they have done, if asked to do so. Commonly they become annoyed if any part of their story is doubted and irritated, out of all proportion, if some minor and relatively unimportant part of their narrative is misunderstood. They seem exasperated at the questioner's stupidity. They will make great play with some trivial mitigating fact and become

indignant if they think some injustice is being done to them, no matter how slight it may be, seeing no incongruity in this when, at about the same time, they are relating some particularly monstrous actions of their own. They can even then appear self-righteous.

(In prison or hospital they are not only disliked by other prisoners or patients who know of their offences but may be at risk from them, and the added fact that they tend to be withdrawn in their relations with others means that they mix poorly with the population of the institution. The greater number are very well behaved whether in prison or in hospital. Herein lies another pitfall, for years of such good behaviour, as a 'model' prisoner or patient, can lead the unwary at a later date to use this as a principal criterion when considering transfer to a less secure institution or even discharge. Much more solid evidence of a fundamental change is required than good conduct, even over a long period, in an environment where there is neither temptation nor opportunity to commit the kind of acts which brought them to the institution in the first place.

Occasionally such a man may be, and remain at times, very violent and dangerous within the institution where he is detained.

Their continuing abnormality may be shown by their desire to learn German, to get books or magazines of the kind that they formerly read or collected dealing with Nazism, sadism or sexual perversions, or by the pictures they draw – not infrequently of battle scenes where warships, tanks and aeroplanes bear swastika markings.

Given the opportunity the sadistic murderer is likely to murder again, and he knows this.

SUMMARY

An attempt is made to describe the sadistic murderer. The description rests on the examination of many men of this kind near the time of the crime and on continuing observation of them over periods of years. It rests only on examination of victims and of scenes of such crimes. In addition, account has been taken of others who show the features of the syndrome and who fantasise committing similar murders although they have not done so.

First published in Medicine and Science, *1970, and reproduced with their permission*

A glance at the characteristics of the individual described in this book will amply bear out Dr Brittain's profile. Among them are:
- Usually introspective and withdrawn, he has few associates and no close friends and enjoys solitary pursuits like reading.
- He feels inadequate and inferior, except in regard to his crimes which make him feel godlike and is likely to offend when he has suffered a loss of self-esteem, such as a loss of job, or being ridiculed by someone especially in a sexual context.
- He can be a hypochondriac and display sqeamishness.
- He is usually under 35, unmarried and of high intelligence.
- He is usually sexually dysfunctional, has usually had little or no experience of normal sexual intercourse and may hate all females.
- He has a strong, ambivalent relationship with his mother, both loving her and hating her. He is often seen as a

'mother's boy' when adult. Sometimes he commits matricide.
- Sometimes the father is excessively punitive and authoritarian.
- The method of killing his victims is almost always strangling which gives him a greater sense of power over his victims, playing with them 'like a cat with a mouse'.
- He can be prim, proper, even prudish, avoiding profanities.
- He can also be sanctimonious and sometimes quotes scriptures.
- He may have books on war and the tying of knots.
- A grandmother, at least in Scotland, is occasionally an important figures.
- They can express strong anti-semitic feelings and marked prejudices against coloured people.
- There may be ropes for self-tying or self-hanging.
- He may also be known to be a particularly tidy person in dress and appearance and very clean.
- This feeling of sexual inferiority as compared with other men may partly explain why many such persons find it difficult to urinate or undress when others are present and so earn themselves a reputation for excessive modesty.
- The planning or contemplation of these acts can make him feel superior to other men, someone special or even godlike.
- Surprising as it may seem, his fantasies, interests and practices do not always make it unacceptable to him and sometimes there is not only a declared interest in it but he may be a church-attender.
- Although these are sexually motivated crimes, sexual intercourse or orgasm does not always occur. Sometimes the murderer masturbates over or beside his victim.

- The victim is commonly found in the position in which the assault took place, without any attempt, for example, to arrange the limbs, but rather as if left in this way as a final degradation. It is as f there were a deliberate attempt to offend modesty.
- Many dress up in female clothing at times.
- A person with the syndrome being described occasionally presents himself as a person with an anxiety state. It may be that the anxiety is a result of resistance to the urge of his murderous drives.
- Their continuing abnormality may be shown by their desire to learn German.

It is possible to list the characteristics commonly found in sadistic murderers and this can be a guide. It is a surprising and at times even a bizarre picture. If it is known, evidence which might otherwise have been overlooked, can be sought and given its proper value.

Of the 24 characteristics I have listed from the profile, the first 16 have already been covered in preceding chapters. The remaining eight will be shown to fit the pattern in the following chapters.

POWER IN THE BLOOD

CHAPTER 6

Acts

But that we write unto them, that they abstain from pollutions of idols, and from fornication, and from things strangled and from blood.
(ACTS, CHAPTER 15, VERSE 20)

During one of my discussion with John X he told me of an afternoon in 1991 when he had had too much to drink and was having difficulty in wending his way home. He called this 'The Good Samaritan' incident. As he neared his home he had stumbled and a woman in her early thirties who arrived on the scene with her daughter, helped him to his door. He thanked the woman for her help and consideration. He went on to tell me he had a very clear picture of her in his mind and she looked very like someone he had known. Since then he had seen her several times and he knew where she lived. He had even learned that she was a widow. From Pateron's description of the woman, I recognised her as a neighbour who I had often seen in the passing although I had never spoken to her.

Several times over the next two years John X made reference to the woman. If he had passed her in the street he would tell me, 'By the way, I saw that woman again today; the one that helped me to my door.' He always used these same words when making reference to these sightings, and

since he had volunteered this information so often, it was obvious he had a long-standing interest in, of fixation with, the woman.

It was precisely this interest of John X's in the 'Good Samaritan' that caused me to look at her more closely. Studying her, I realised that in height, appearance and hair colouring, she resembled the photograph of his mother but, more interestingly, she resembled the 'Bible John' victims. On browsing through a book on the murders which contained photographs of the victims, I was surprised and shaken when I saw that Jemima McDonald, in her photograph, was the exact double of the woman. Was this why John X had had such a clear picture of her in his mind when he said she reminded him of someone he had known? Was it conjecture on my part? Somehow I had a feeling about it and decided to keep a watch on the situation.

Nine months after I had moved away from Glasgow, a friend telephoned me from a public telephone box in the area of the West End where I used to live. As we chatter he said he could see John X walking up the road towards him. I asked him to call John X over to the telephone box so that I could speak to him. He did this and when John X came on the line I asked him how he was keeping. He told me that for the past few days he had not been feeling well; that he had been feeling agitated and nervous. 'What do you think has caused it?' I asked.

'I don't know. It started on Wednesday afternoon. I had drunk half a bottle of whisky when I became agitated and anxious. I left the house and it was about 1.30 in the afternoon. I walked down the lane behind my flat, then down the back lane of the adjacent street. I was halfway down this back lane when I suddenly became rigid. I couldn't move and my legs were paralysed.'

'What happened then?' I asked.

'I started to shout for help. I just couldn't move. I couldn't go forward or I couldn't go back. I was rooted to the spot with sweat pouring from my forehead. Someone must have heard my shouts for help, as after a while an ambulance arrived but they refused to take me as they could find nothing wrong with me and they said I smelled of drink. Eventually a police car arrived and took me to the police station where they held me in a cell until teatime and then they let me go.'

I felt that I had got so in tune with the workings of this man's mind that I knew exactly at whose gate he had stopped!

I was sure it was the gate of the woman who had helped him to his door. I telephoned a neighbour in the area who knew this woman as she lived only a few doors away from her. Without going into detail, I asked her to find out what she could about the incident. By chance, a few days later, she met the woman in the bank and the woman confirmed that indeed John X had been right at her back gate, hanging on to it as he called for help. She had gone out to ask the man if she could do anything for him and he had asked her to call an ambulance, which she had done, confirming that it had in fact been the police who had taken him away. She said it was all so strange, recounting that she had once helped this same man to his door when he was drunk. One of the characteristics R.P. Brittain had written bout in *The Sadistic Murderer* came to mind: 'The person with the syndrome being described occasionally presents as a person with an anxiety state. It may be the anxiety is a result of resistance to the urge of his murderous drives.' Did this unsuspecting 'Good Samaritan', unaware of her resemblance to one of the victims of 'Bible John', trigger that urge? I was sure there

was more to this than he would care to admit. Had he been watching her and known she would be at home? Was it his age that was now curbing his murderous urges? I believe he was not as drunk as he made out when she had helped him to his door. He could remember her clearly and had found out where she lived. Was his fixation with her established before then? This man was calculating, intelligent and cunning.

A few months after this incident i visited John X and when I walked into his sitting-room an open Bible lay on his coffee table. I could see that he had underlined verses and when he saw me glancing at it he immediately closed the Bible and put it away. It was the King James version and I knew that somehow I had to get to see what he had underlined.

Five years had passed since I first met John X, and I had an idea that this Bible cold yield some intriguing answers. I formulated a plan which I hoped would make it possible to get to see this Bible with the verses that had been underlined. With a friend, I travelled to Glasgow, taking a bottle of whisky for John X, knowing this gift would be welcome as he was partial to a wee dram. He was at home and we were invited in. Knowing it was one of his weaknesses I filled his glass. I sipped my drink slowly, making it last, while I kept refilling his glass every time he drained it. In an hour he was relaxed and I then led him into a deliberate argument by insisting that there were two separate Bibles, the Old Testament and the New Testament, each within its own cover as a separate Bible. The ploy worked. He went straight to his bookcase and produced his King James Bible, placing it in front of me on his fireside table. He was triumphant as he did this, announcing: 'You've lost the argument.'

I pretended defeat saying, 'You are right. would you mind

if I have a look at it?'

'Help yourself,' he replied, and I slipped it into my inside coat pocket, continuing to distract him by filling his glass again. I had one more task to accomplish before leaving. I needed a sample of his handwriting so as there would be no doubt as to the authenticity of any written comments in the Bible. Pointing to the wall-plaque which bore the religious saying 'He will look after those that I have committed unto Him', I pretended I was interested in getting the same plaque. He told me where it could be purchased and I asked him to write down the address of the shop and the saying on the plaque, in case I forgot it. When I left, I had both the Bible and a sample of his handwriting.

The following day, being Sunday, I had plenty of time to peruse the verses he had underlined and the comments he had noted. The passages had been underlined in red and blue ink. It made chilling reading. Passages referring to harlots, the shedding of blood, whoredoms and the wife that 'committeth adultery', he had underlined throughout. Other passages included *That they keep themselves from things offered to idols, and from blood, and from strangled, and from fornication.* He had marked other passages referring to *the destruction of the sinful.* In Joshua 7, he had underlined *neither will I be with you any more, except ye destroy the accursed among you.*

A characteristic from *The Sadistic Murderer* fitted aptly: 'Surprising as it may seem, his fantasies, interests and practices do not always make religion unacceptable to him and sometimes there is not only a declared interest in but he may be a church-attender.'

Was he using the Bible as a manual for his activities? In Psalms 56 he had marked, *In God I will praise His word, in God I have put my trust; I will not fear what flesh can do*

unto me. On one page, in red ink, he had written 'MURDER' in the margin next to the text which read *And when the blood of thy martyr Stephen was shed. I also was standing by, and consenting unto his death, and kept the raiment of them that slew him.*

Most of the victims of 'Bible John' had been stripped of their clothing and either it was never found or else it was found scattered miles from the scene. In *The Sadistic Murderer*, Dr Brittain wrote, 'many dress up in female clothing at times', and 'transvested while they indulge in various sexual fantasies'. Had John X underlined the passage *and kept the raiment of them* to show his perversion in cross-dressing and sexual fantasies? had the killer, 'Bible John', stunned his victim and dressed quickly in some of their clothes before killing them, or did he take items of clothing, or handbags, to fantasise later? A grim warning was clear in his underlining of this chapter: *And I say unto you my friends, be not afraid of them that kill the bloody, and after that have no more that they can do. But I will forewarn you whom ye shall fear: Fear him which after he hath killed, hath power to cast into hell: yea I say unto you; Fear him.*

The next passage John X had underlined was macabre, as it stood out when I saw it. A chilling note beside that passage read, 'Dundee 1978–80 . . . *O sing, unto the Lord a new song for He hath done marvellous things: His right hand and His holy arm hath gotten Him victory.* A characteristic mentioned in *The Sadistic Murderer* fits in here. 'The planning or contemplation of these acts can make him feel superior to other men; someone special, or even godlike.' Was John X using his Bible as a secret, cryptic diary? He had said he had been to Dundee for a change of venue!

More horrific was the underlined passage, *Because of the multitude of whoredoms of the well-favoured harlot the*

mistress of witchcrafts, that selleth nations through her whoredoms, and families through her witchcrafts.

Behold, I am against three saith the Lord of hosts; and I will discover they skirts upon thy face, and I will shew the nations thy nakedness, and the kingdom thy shame.. Several of the victims had been stripped naked. Did the latter sentence also cryptically refer to the sanitary towel under Helen Puttock's armpit, and to the other victims who had been menstruating when they were murdered? By underlining these passages in particular, John X surely shows his conformity to the type of person Dr Brittain is profiling, as illustrated by these observations.

'The victim is commonly found in the position in which the assault took place without any attempt, for example, to arrange the limbs, but rather as if left in this way as a final degradation. It is as if there were a deliberate attempt to offend modesty.' Further passages underlined are *Behold, all souls are mine; as the soul of the father so also the soul of the son is mine: the soul that sinneth, it shall die.* The next passage was underlined in parts. *All his transgressions that he hath committed they shall not be mentioned unto him; in his righteousness that he hath done he shall live.*

Many more passages had been underlined which concentrated on adultery, sex, death, blood, the unclean and whores. Other passages underlined referred to justification for murder, forgiveness and laws which forgave murder in certain circumstances. The many years I had spent studying John X had given me the ability to interpret his underlining of passages in his secret diary/Bible.

In fact there is a strong possibility that a slip of the tongue he had made while talking to a neighbour could be interpreted as a reference to the murder of the first victim, Patricia Docker. This incident occurred after I had moved

away from Glasgow.

The neighbour, a close friend, told me he had called at her door. She could not understand why he should call to see her as she did not know him, having only met him once or twice as he happened to be in the garage when she had stopped to say hello to be briefly. Actually, she confided later that she had cut these visits short because John X 'gave her the creeps'.

She had arrived home in the afternoon and on opening the gate was astonished and aghast to see John X there, talking to her daughter's boyfriend on the doorstep. He had obviously been drinking and asked her if she had seen me recently. 'Yes, he called here four days ago,' she told him, 'but I haven't heard from him since.' She felt uneasy as she sensed his enquiry was merely an excuse, and she had a distinct feeling that he was prying, trying to find out what I was up to and also to discover if she knew anything of my suspicions of him. She was alarmed, since I had outlined parts of the story to her over a period of time. Her daughter's boyfriend, unaware who the man was, had gone back into the house, leaving them alone. My friend related that John X stood facing her, his camel hair coat unbuttoned and with both hands thrust into the pockets, arms stretched out to the sides, so that the coat was held wide open, revealing his neat suit beneath. He was unsteady on his feet, swaying slightly and staggering backwards, his breath smelling of drink. He had been enquiring after me and my health, making reference to my recent stay in hospital. The topic of hospitals having been raised, he went on to talk about nurses, touching on their assumed reputation as being sexually permissive. Then he announced with a leering expression on his face, 'I went out with a nurse once! Do you think the ladies would still fancy me?'

POWER IN THE BLOOD

'Not this lady!' she told him curtly, wondering all the while how she was going to get rid of him. She was relieved when, at this point, her daughter called down that there was a telephone call for her, so she excused herself, and closed the door leaving John X to pick his way gingerly down the pebbled pathway and out of the gate. She telephoned me to tell me about the incident, saying, 'It gave me a really weird feeling having him there in my garden, Donald.' When recounting this incident she emphasised that she couldn't understand why he had suddenly told her he had once gone out with a nurse.

In my conversations with John X over the past few years he had never mentioned having gone out with a nurse. He had, in fact, told me that he had never had a girlfriend, but that, 'There was a bus conductress who I am sure fancied me, but it sort of died.' This is explained in a previous chapter about the veiled hint to Helen Puttock's murder. Was this mention of 'I went out with a nurse once' another cryptic reference to murder – the murder of Patricia Docker who was a nurse? Whoever was out with her on the night of her murder was out with her once and once only and it led to her death.

* * *

One of the final pieces of the jigsaw fell into place a week later when I called to see John X again. I was astonished to see a bookcase which had previously been filled with religious books now stacked with books on learning German. I was really amazed and when I asked him where he had got them, he replied, 'Oh, I've always had them' I kept them hidden.' I didn't ask him why. In his psychological profile of the serial killer, Dr Brittain had explained that, 'their continuing abnormality may be shown by their desire

to learn German'.

Towards the end of my tape recording of John X, he evidently becomes annoyed at my persistence about the slip knot and how he used it when he tried to kill his father. A characteristic from the profile reads, 'Commonly they become annoyed if any part of their story is doubted and irritated out of all proportion if some minor and relatively unimportant part of their narrative is misunderstood'.

Here I was with a powerful, thought-provoking study of the unsolved 'Bible John' murders. The study was remarkable in that everything could be connected circumstantially but despite this the police showed no interest. It seemed as if, as one door shut in my face, another one slammed! It brought to mind the case of the Yorkshire Ripper, Peter Sutcliffe. The officers involved in the investigation were misled by the tape-recording of a man with a Geordie accent. During that investigation the police had been approached by three individuals: a close friend of Sutcliffe's, a private investigator and a police traffic sergeant. Each had named Sutcliffe but their approach fell on stony ground. The police had adopted a blinkered attitude as to who they were looking for. When Sutcliffe was apprehended, it was only then that the folly of their direction emerged. In fact, a five pound note that had been issued to the firm where Sutcliffe worked and actually issued to Sutcliffe in his wages, turned out to be the very note recovered from the property of one of the victims. It had been one of several hundred notes whose serial numbers were traced to the haulage firm where he worked. Furthermore, the officer who interviewed him was unaware that a bootprint taken from the murder scene of one of Sutcliffe's victims matched the boots that Sutcliffe was actually wearing as he was being interviewed by this officer.

All this was overlooked, otherwise the lives of many other young women could have been saved. As a parallel to 'Bible John's' quoting of scripture, Sutcliffe reported hearing God telling him to kill prostitutes.

My only recourse was once again to approach the investigative journalist to whom I had spoken before. i contacted him and asked if he would look at John X's Bible and hear me out once more. He agreed and when we met I outlined the further developments since I had seen him two years previously. Unlike the Serious Crime Squad, he could see the significance of the details I had accumulated. Because of the apparent lack of interest shown by officialdom, I indicated to him that I was prepared to go public. Having dealt with numerous investigations over the years which had led to exposés of criminal activities and the ultimate imprisonment of some of the individuals involved, he knew the importance of the checking and validating of evidence before going into print.

He recognised the sincerity of my claims and set to work to check out my story. Many weeks later he contacted me to confirm that his paper would print an article on my claims. It was circulated on 12 and 13 April 1995, laying out on three pages on both days, a condensed version of my claims. The report included an interview the journalist had conducted with John X. This is the report of that interview:

> The scripture-quoting man, branded 'Bible John', freely admits he used prostitutes. His bookcase is packed with bibles, psalm books and religious pamphlets. The wall of his council flat carries quotations from the bible. He regularly quotes short texts from the bible. Yet the same man confessed: 'I have used prostitutes. I have gone with them. And I did have a relationship with one who I went with

regularly. I had a regard for her.'

In an interview in his house the 61-year-old, grey-haired bachelor, who has never married, talked about himself.

'I went to the Barrowland twice. I know about "Bible John" and Helen Puttock because i lived near to where she was found.'

He talked for almost two hours about the factors that have meant he has twice been interviewed in the 'Bible John' investigation.

The suspect would not refer to Helen's killing as 'murder'. He calls it the 'Helen Puttock incident'.

He was asked why the police had interviewed him about Helen's murder. The man replied that police had traced him to his bed-sit in the West End. And he claimed he had been interviewed by the police because he had lived in the area and fitted the information about 'Bible John' as supplied by Jeannie Williams, Helen's sister. The picture was of a well-spoken, well-dressed, upright, religious man.

He said: 'A person who goes to church is usually well dressed, and in conversation they will use a quotation from the Bible. They acquire a polish in their speech that they didn't otherwise have.'

And he said there was a Bible on the table when the detectives came into his room. He said: 'I told them that I had been at church on that night. At the Park Church, at the corner of Park Road and Woodside Road.' But he agreed he could have taken a taxi to the dance hall after the service.

When the suspect was asked if anything was troubling him he replied; 'am I at peace? The thing is death is near.'

He was asked what the problem would be for a man coping with the problems 'Bible John' must carry and he replied: 'I remember a minister pointing out there is good cause to believe murder can be forgiven.'

Asked if he took a taxi to the dancing he replied: 'I may well have taken a taxi. In those days I took a taxi frequently.'

Did he take a taxi home from the Barrowland dancing?

'I only went to the Barrowland dancing *twice*. I don't drive. I can't drive.'

Asked if he had ever received hospital treatment he replied: 'I was diagnosed as schizophrenic.'

He was asked about an attempt to strangle his father: 'Did you try to kill your father by strangling him with a rope?' The man answered: 'The noose slipped and he survived.'

When asked about the 'Bible John' murders he said: 'I didn't do it. I like to think you have eliminated me.'

Not only were there many coincidences and circumstances pointing to a connection between John X and these distant events, but in Robert P. Brittain's *The Sadistic Murderer*, most of the characteristics it profiles fit John X like a glove.

The dossier, the Bible and the tape-recording were handed to the police.

POWER IN THE BLOOD

CHAPTER 7

Lamentations

They have wandered as blind men in the streets; they have polluted themselves with blood, so that men could not touch their garments.
(LAMENTATIONS, CHAPTER 4, VERSE 14)

Psychiatrists agree that a person must be of high intelligence or possess a great deal of base cunning to get away with murder again and again. Serial killers are difficult to catch as they have both intelligence and the ability to evade detection and are also capable of acting normally after committing their crimes. In the majority of murders, arrests can be made fairly quickly, as the perpetrator is either a relative, neighbour, or an acquaintance of the victim, whereas the serial killer is a rarer breed. His premeditated planning and murder of a complete stranger, seemingly without motive, presents the police with a formidable task.

A manhunt on the scale of that mounted at the time of the 'Bible John' murders had not been seen in Glasgow since the 1950s when the murderer Peter Manuel was at large.

Manuel, while he was extremely cunning, was also loud and boastful, certainly a sadistic murderer, but he lacked the intelligence of 'Bible John' and this factor led to his downfall.

His catalogue of rape and murder began on a quiet

country road in 1946 when he brutally assaulted and raped a young woman. He was soon caught and sentenced to eight years' imprisonment on the rape charge. By 1952 he was free again. In 1955 he attacked another girl in a country lane and once more he was arrested, but the case against him was found not proven. Manuel openly boasted to an associate that he was guilty. Tragically, nine people were to die at his hands.

Anne Neilands, the first of his murder victims, was 17 years old. She left her home in East Kilbride in the early evening of 2 January 1956 to keep a date with a young soldier she had met at the dancing. Her route had taken her along a quiet path and a narrow country road. On 4 January she was found dead in a small wood not far off her route and her belongings had been scattered over a wide area. This fact, together with her injuries, showed that she had run through fields and ditches, through a barbed wire fence and hedging before being caught and bludgeoned to death. She had not been sexually assaulted but her dark blue knickers were missing.

On the morning of Monday, 17 September 1956, a Mrs Watt, her daughter, and her sister, Mrs Brown, were found shot dead in their bungalow in Burnside, Lanarkshire. They had been shot through the head as they slept. Mr William Watt had left on 9 September for a fishing holiday in Argyll, 90 miles away. He was arrested and charged with the murder of his wife, his daughter and his sister-in-law, and was remanded in custody.

Meanwhile, on 2 October 1956, Manuel was sentence to 18 months' imprisonment for burglary and sent to Barlinnie prison where Mr Watt was serving his sentence. He had the effrontery to contact Watt's lawyer to tell him that he knew who had killed the Watt family. He told the lawyer he knew

the man who had committed the murders, giving certain details of the interior of the Watts' house which was enough to convince the lawyer that Manuel had been inside it. Subsequently Manuel was investigated although no charge was brought against him but Mr Watt was freed. When Manuel was released a year later he contacted Mr Watt and related the same story he had told the lawyer convincing him that Manuel had indeed murdered his family.

A Newcastle taxi driver was found dead in his taxi on a remote country road. He had been shot through the head and his throat had been cut. It was 8 December 1957 and there was evidence that Manuel had been in Newcastle that day.

On 28 December, 18-year-old Isabelle Cooke left her home in Mount Vernon to go dancing. She didn't get there, nor did she return. When her clothes were found in the River Calder, the police feared the worst. Later, when Manuel was arrested on other murder charges, he showed the police the shallow grave where he had buried her.

On 6 January 1958 a Mr Smart, his wife and 11-year-old son were found murdered in their bungalow. They had been shot as they lay asleep and had lain dead for six days before their bodies were discovered, the reason being that the curtains of their home had been drawn and opened each day to give the impression that someone was at home. Manuel was cunning enough to come and go without being seen. Nevertheless, he was arrested on 14 January 1958 and found guilty on overwhelming evidence and hanged several months later.

There were similarities between the Manuel murders and those of 'Bible John', in that the men themselves were loners; in some cases after killing their victims they removed all or part of the clothing; sometimes there was no evidence of sexual assault.

There were also differences. While Manuel used cunning in the execution of his crimes, his low intelligence led to his capture: on the other hand, 'Bible John''s high intelligence enabled him to avoid detection and he is still at liberty to this day.

When the series of murders of young women took place in Glasgow in the late 1960s, all following the same *modus operandi*, the press jumped to the conclusions that they were the work of one individual and they were responsible for dubbing him 'Bible John'. These so-called 'Bible John' murders have never been acknowledged by the police as the work of one man. Did Scotland have an intelligent serial killer who first struck in Glasgow and later moved further afield to Edinburgh and Dundee, cunningly enjoying his game of evading the police and capture?

It is in Russia where another comparison can be made to the 'Bible John' murders. Andrei Romanovich Chikatilo, a sadistic murderer, evaded capture for 12 years. Chikatilo, a former teacher, whose job as a supply clerk enabled him to travel widely, sometimes with overnight stays, murdered 55 people. He was a quiet, introspective individual with a prudish morality who associated with prostitutes although he despised them as loose and promiscuous. At the time when Chikatilo's later murders were committed, one of them was mistakenly attributed to an innocent man who was accused and executed for the crime. These later murders sparked off the largest murder hunt that Russia had known.

As with the 'Bible John' murders, they were not acknowledged by the police as the work of one man. It was only when the Soviet Union's Department for Special Importance became involved that it was agreed that they had a serial killer at large. They copied the FBI's approach and drew up a psychological profile of their serial killer. Half a

million people were interviewed in the manhunt for Chikatilo. He was arrested in September 1984 by two plainclothes detectives who had been observing him behaving oddly trying to pick up women. When they arrested him he had an eight-inch kitchen knife in his brief case. The detectives believed they had caught the serial killer but a blood test showed that Chikatilo's type A blood did not match the semen type AB found on his previous victims. No one thought to check Chikatilo's semen type, since at that time it was accepted as a scientific fact that blood and semen always matched. Since then, however, scientists have discovered that in rare instances this is untrue. Chikatilo was freed and went on to murder 21 more victims over the next six years until he was finally arrested in December 1990. Six hundred police officers were assigned to the case, which had been dubbed 'The Forest Strip Killer' because of Chikatilo's habit of burying his victims in strips of woodland alongside railway tracks. Eventually the perseverance of these 600 police officers paid off.

A police sergeant based at a railway station in Doleskhoz watched as a man emerged from the woods and proceeded to wash his hands and shoes at a water hydrant. The man had a bandaged finger and blood on his cheek. The police sergeant asked for his documents and discovered that the man was Andrei Chikatilo, who, unknown to the policeman, had just murdered a 22-year-old woman in the woods from which he had emerged. Chikatilo, calm and unconcerned, was allowed to go. Six days later the police sergeant's report landed on the desk of a murder squad officer. The name seemed familiar to the officer in charge and while checking Andrei Chikatilo's file from his arrest in 1984, when he had been released because of the discrepancy between his blood and semen type, the officer remembered recent Japanese

research which claimed that this was possible in an individual although very rare. The officer ordered a search of the woods where the body of the young woman was discovered and Chikatilo was caught at last. The psychological profile that had been drawn up turned out to be an accurate description of the murderer.

It was known that 'Bible John' had alighted from a bus at Gray Street and had not travelled on the late-night ferry to Govan. Therefore, any suspect fitting the description, who had reddish-fair hair, was well spoken, and when officers visited his home had an open Bible on his table and was living in Clouston Street, less than a mile and a half from where the murderer got off the bus, should have been a p[rime suspect and placed on an identity parade. Did the officer who interviewed John X have the preconceived idea that the murderer would be a brutish gorilla of a man and when he spoke to John X, who would have been glib and calm (like Chikatilo), eliminated him from the enquiry too readily?

One of the problems with serial killers is just how ordinary they are. The manhunt was so massive and the volume of evidence so great, it is understandable that facts can be overlooked. There were no computers available to the police in 1969 and all records had to be written up painstakingly by hand. There is no doubt that had computers been an option they would have proved invaluable in the collating of data and evidence, making it a much less time-consuming activity and at the same time allowing officers to concentrate on more important business. However, like the DNA test, computers are only as good as the people who use them and one should never believe in their total infallibility. With the advances in technology such as 'Holmes, the national police computer and genetic fingerprinting, aids in

detection are now far superior, but mistakes can still be made.

In July 1987, on a typical west of Scotland summer night – wet and windy – Brian Kelly was out drinking with his pals in Largs, the small seaside town where he lived. They visited many of the pubs in the town and in the course of the night he had at least 12 drinks.

The spree over, Brian walked home a distance of about three-quarters of a mile from the town centre and as he came closer to his house he could see that the lights were on. This was very unusual as his family were normally in bed when he came home from a night out. When his wife Anne heard him walking up the garden path to the front door, she drew back the curtain and looked out. Brian could see that Anne was on the phone and he immediately felt apprehensive. He was sure it would be some bad news about his father. As soon as he got in he asked Anne if there was something wrong with his dad. 'No,' said Anne, explaining that it was their friend, Susan, who had just told her that a man had broken into the house through a window and raped her. Brian was very shocked and fell back against the wall saying, 'My God!'

Brian Kelly was a policeman in Largs and the next day at the police station he was asked, as part of routine enquiries checking all men who had been out late the previous evening, to give a statement. DNA evidence found at the scene of the crime led to Brian being charged with the attack. Brian said that he couldn't believe it. It was devastating, especially since he had nothing to do with it; he had left the pub, said goodbye to his friends and headed home, but the police claimed later that it would have been possible for Brian to double back and walk the half mile to Susan's house where he had raped her. Those involved in preparing the case

for the prosecution had a very major problem. Although Susan had spent a considerable time with her attacker, she never identified Brian. She had stated that her attacker was clean smelling, whereas Brian must have smelt strongly of drink from the amount he had drunk that night. A voice identification parade was held and Susan naturally recognised Brian's voice but she picked out someone else as her attacker. The pubic hair that was found was not Brian's. In fact there seemed to be no evidence against him. Susan had remained friends with both Anne and Brian for some time after the crime. How then could Brian be brought to court? The prosecution had one piece of key evidence – the DNA test.

The Home Office labs weren't able to get any results from the samples taken from the scene of the crime so they sent two samples, one from the nightdress and one from the dressing-gown, to the UK division of Cellmark to see if they could obtain any results. Cellmark couldn't get a match from Brian's DNA or from Susan's nightdress. They claimed, however, to have found a match from the dressing-gown sample. Four separate probes were claimed in court to have produced a match and such a match, the jury were told, would happen only once in 100,000 times by chance. Susan still would not identify Brian as her attacker. Despite the fact that there was no other real evidence against Brian, it was science that mattered.

A majority verdict of 'guilty' was declared and Brian was taken to Barlinnie in Glasgow, one of Scotland's toughest prisons, to serve a six-year sentence. 'I was in such a state of shock, the depths of despair, I think,' said Brian recently, remembering his feelings at the time. He continued, 'You're hoping, constantly hoping that it's just a nightmare, that the thing's going to end, that someone's going to come to the

door of your cell the next day and say, "It's all been a big mistake, you're going home".' But the next day came and went, and the next and no one ever did come, for despite all the evidence in Brian's favour, the DNA tests looked conclusive.

Simon Ford, an expert in DNA testing in America, agreed to look at the DNA evidence produced at the trial. He was so concerned by what he found that he flew to Glasgow to meet Donald Finlay QC, one of Scotland's top advocates, who had taken up Brian's case. Cellmark's report said that there was a match and the precautions taken were such that it was impossible for this to be a false positive and they estimated that this particular match would occur at a frequency of one in 100,000. This report just doesn't tell the whole story. The first concern was that the Kelly test results did not have clear marker tracks. Further documents from Cellmark confirmed that the human DNA mark was either not run or did not produce a result. Since 1989 this type of evidence has been inadmissible in American courts. The sample from the scene of the crime and Brian's DNA were loaded in adjacent tracks. Occasionally, when samples are loaded on the same gel you can get spillage from one lane to the adjacent lane and spillage could mean that a false match was produced. There is no doubt that the jury were influenced by the DNA and we now know this evidence may be fundamentally flawed.

Of course, that was a few years ago now but the same test is still used by many police forces. However, the new National Database uses the PCR test for more accuracy. This test was invented on paper and as a concept it is 100 per cent accurate. Kary Mullis won the Nobel Prize for his work on this test and he explains that it can be used on very small samples but its very accuracy increases the problem of

contamination. In the recent O.J. Simpson trial the DNA analysis (using the PCR test) on stains on the pavement and a glove was at the centre of the case. Indeed this was the primary evidence against him.

Kary Mullis advised the defence team in the trial that samples have to be dealt with in the strictest of conditions to avoid contamination. When blood was taken from OJ in the police labs, some of the blood squirted up into the air out of the tube. Mullis explained that DNA can dry and form a dust and this dust can be stirred up like any other dust. The scenario then was that the police lab was full of OJ's DNA in the form of a dust. Mullis claimed that when the samples from the pavement were taken, very little, if any, human DNA would be left as the samples were, by then, so degraded. Then the samples were put in the back of a van where they lay for seven hours on a very hot day. This would cause the DNA to be eaten up by bacteria. The police were ecstatic when they got a match but as OJ's DNA was floating in the air in the lab, contamination could have taken place. This does not mean, of course, that there wasn't a match but that the evidence was put in doubt and the jury has to keep in mind at all times that evidence must be beyond reasonable doubt.

Even 26 years after the 'Bible John' murders, had any body fluids been discovered by the scene of crime officers at the time, they could still be DNA tested. Providing any such specimens had been kept clean and dry r deep frozen and had not been contaminated they could still be matched to a suspect today.

Why was no one ever apprehended for the 'Bible John' murders? This question has been asked countless times, not only by the public in general but by the police themselves. The debate as to whether the killings were the work of one

man raged on, splitting opinion among the senior ranks of the Glasgow Police. It was the press who suggested the link publicly by dubbing the killings 'the Bible John murders'. The idea of a serial killer operating in Glasgow was rejected by the police.

The police in the United States were familiar with the phenomenon of the serial killer and it was about this time, prompted by the high incidence of crimes committed by serious offenders such as the serial killer Ted Bundy, that the Americans developed interstate intelligence information. When a crime is committed evidence gathered from the scene is translated into behavioural characteristics, enabling an analyst to build an 'offender profile'. This was the beginning of the Americans' Behavioural Sciences Unit. Although this is used in connection with crimes other than murder it has proved invaluable for American crime fighters in the apprehension of serial killers for, even if a serial killer crosses state lines to commit his crimes, all data on murders is fed into the same computer and common indicators are then discovered.

A sadistic killer's modus operandi tells psychologists into which of several categories he might fall. The two main ones are the 'organised Nonsocial' killer and the 'Disorganised Asocial' killer. The 'Organised Nonsocial' killer shrewdly presents a façade of warmth and friendliness towards society while secretly committing his carefully planned and methodical crimes which he knows will shock that same society; indeed, this is part of his aim. He is likely to be on the look-out for a victim and the ideal opportunity when it would be safe for him to commit his crime undetected. The 'Disorganised Asocial' individual, on the other hand, is a loner, a friendless outsider who feels rejected but who murders in a more controlled and less methodical way and is

then likely to abandon the body making no attempt to hide it. In contrast, the 'Organised Nonsocial' type may, in an attempt to control matters further, even go so far as to remove the body from the murder scene and then later put it somewhere else where it is likely to be found, whereupon he may follow news of its discovery and the ensuing murder enquiry with excitement.

What would the American crime fighters make of 'Bible John'? His solitariness and his feelings of alienation coupled with his practice of leaving the murder scene without trying to conceal the body would suggest he fitted the disorganised category, yet he was carefully calculating in the extreme, a fact borne out by the way he planned his strategy and selected his victims. Furthermore, he actually felt compelled to arrange the bodies and clothing of his victims in a certain way, following instructions, as he interpreted them from particular passages in the Bible. Without a doubt, then, 'Bible John' was an organised killer. If he had been a disorganised type, how did he control his violent urges until he had lured his victims to a suitable killing ground? To single out the perfect victim, he chose to go to dance halls, where the informal, anonymous setting was ideal for his purpose. His apparently casual and unhurried approach to female dancers was friendly and chatty, his conversation dotted with biblical references and then, after gaining their confidence, he would escort them home, cunningly awaiting his chance to strike, Afterwards, 'Bible John' carried on what appeared to be a normal public life, inconspicuously going about his business more or less as usual.

The late Professor Keith Simpson, a renowned forensic pathologist, pointed out that although many murders come to the notice of the police there are many more that do not. The question then arises whether or not 'Bible John' killed others

that n one knows about. It is possible but one of the characteristics of his psyche is that he thrives on the knowledge that his crimes have been discovered and any undiscovered murder may have meant for him an anti-climax in his deadly game.

Perhaps intuition alone has prompted me to continue in my observations of John X for so long. But that is as valid a reason for doing so as any other. The late William Muncie, formerly Assistant Chief Constable of Strathclyde Police, pointed out: 'Mammals and birds have extra built-in senses. The wonder of all migratory birds is the cuckoo. Fostered as an egg, it never sees its parents, yet alone and for the first time in its life it will leave this country and, with in-born navigational sense, find its way to Africa, its winter quarters. Even the homing instinct of a racing pigeon defies explanation, while dogs, and even more so cats, have been known to find their way back home on a journey of many miles from a place in which they had never before set foot.' Intuition, instinct, sixth-sense, call it what you will, it led me on an uncharted journey of discovery, the outcome of which I could never in my wildest dreams have envisaged.

At this point I have to reconsider if in fact, through an overactive imagination, I have painted a totally believable if fanciful scenario around an innocent party, causing him unnecessary distress. If that is the case, then I do indeed have a dangerous mind.

There have been other suspects over the years. In December 1977 the *Daily Record* published a story which claimed that a man suspected by many senior policemen to be 'Bible John' had been interviewed about the unsolved murders of four women in Scotland that year. The writer, Arnot McWhinnie, went on to say that he had known the identity of the man, an electrician from a town in the west of

Scotland, for as long as seven years but he was sworn to secrecy as the man had been sent to a mental hospital after admitting to the vicious rape of a young woman. Three years later, McWhinnie published a sensational interview with the man in which he denied being 'Bible John' although he understood why police suspected him and added: 'I have an innocent explanation for everything.' One such thing was the fact that he had been to a dentist to have his two front teeth removed; he claimed this was because of a football injury.

In January 1983, there was a renewed flurry of interest in the 'Bible John' story when a heating engineer called Harry Wylie suddenly went public with his private suspicions about his one-time best friend, David Henderson, who had gone to live in Holland in 1970. In their younger days, in the late sixties, they had often gone to Barrowland ballroom together – though they had not always left together – and Harry had long found David to be 'the double of the "Bible John" drawing'. So convinced did Wylie become with this thought that he even hired private detectives to check out Henderson, 'hoping they would prove him wrong; but as their investigation went on, the more coincidences kept cropping up'.

I do have material pointers provided freely or unintentionally by none other than John X himself. I have spent four years keenly observing the man's behaviour and reactions, posing leading questions, engineered to elicit anticipated responses, weighing up and evaluating each new piece of the jigsaw. It could be said that much of the information that came to light falls within the sphere of coincidence and a few isolated coincidences could be dismissed as tenuous; but when there are so many coincidences that they shape up so that the pieces all interlock to form a clear picture, then surely that picture

deserves further consideration.

An example of one such coincidence is the fact that my suspect John X, long before I had ever met him, was one of the people to have been interviewed by the police at the time of the 'Bible John' murders, but John X has not made a spirited defence of himself after the appearance of the newspaper article on my story. He has gone to ground.

POWER IN THE BLOOD

CHAPTER 8

Exodus

Thou hast set our iniquities before thee, our secret sins in the light of thy countenance.
(PSALMS, CHAPTER 9, VERSE 8)

It is 27 years since 'Bible John' claimed his first victim. He is Scotland's most notorious serial killer and has remained at large, eluding capture in the longest manhunt known in this country. The whole of Glasgow felt the weight of the oppressive dark shadow he had cast over the city as it was turned inside out in the search for this infamous killer. Mothers warned their children not to stay out late, saying '"Bible John" will get you!'. His name was on everyone's lips. Many young women even stopped going to the dance halls and those brave enough to keep on going declined dancing partners' offers to escort them home. Men who resembled 'Bible John' found themselves being stopped in the street and invited to the police station where they were asked to account for their whereabouts at the time of the third murder. Some were accosted so often by different officers that they were provided with an official letter clearing them from the enquiry, which stated, 'I am certified as not being "Bible John"'.

People's imaginations ran riot, so much so that they fancied they could see him lurking in unlit alleys and

darkened shop doorways or keeping to the shadows of tree-lined streets smoking an Embassy cigarette before discarding it and moving on to select another victim. The police were snowed under by reports of sightings: 'He's my stepfather, I never liked him. It must be him.' 'He's on the Inverness train.' 'He's in the Curlers Bar.' 'He's on a bus.' 'I work beside him.' These were some of the many thousands of leads police officers had to follow up. They sifted through all of those leads, conducted interviews, eliminating some suspects, grilling others. Churchgoers on Sundays, sitting in the pews, would notice a red-headed man sitting in front of them and where previously they would have given him no more than a cursory glance, this time their gaze would linger a little longer as they wondered . . . Every man with red hair was the butt of the question: 'Is it you, are you "Bible John"?' The question would be asked in a lighthearted way, but half-seriously at the same time. Even 'Bible John' himself would have been asked the very same question by his few unsuspecting associates and he would have replied reassuringly in his well-spoken west of Scotland tones: 'Ha, ha, ha, don't be silly.'

'Yes, he's just an nice ordinary guy,' they would think and never mention it again. Even to this day the police still have at least two callers a day claiming they know who 'Bible John' is.

The man alighted from the bus and headed for the dark, tree-lined Kelvin Way. His stride though brisk was unhurried as he kept to the shadows, nor did he glance furtively over his shoulder. He was on God's business, his twin obsessions being murder and religion. There were no terrible flashbacks of his hideous deeds; he had become indifferent, without remorse or conscience; already he'd blanked it from his mind; had been someone else. In his jacket pocket he

gripped the Bible that had been there since he left the church meeting earlier that evening. The feel of it reassured him. His hands didn't tremble when he put his door key in the lock. He opened the door, closed it behind him and calmly removed the Bible from his pocket, placing it on his table. Opening it he flicked through the well-thumbed pages to the chapter he had read earlier. Lifting a pen, he underlined the verse: *All his transgressions that he hath committed they shall not be mentioned unto him.* He retired to bed and slept well.

Months later the dancers slowly trickled back to the dance venues. Thursday nights were a particular favourite for the over-25s, the older sort, some of whom had left their husbands or wives at home. As the throngs took to the floor when the band struck up in the heady atmosphere and excitement of the Barrowland Ballroom, more than a few married dancers slipped their wedding rings off their fingers. The Barrowland had gained a certain notoriety over the years for this very practice. The police continued to mingle with the dancers but they were met with a stony silence. A lot of the dancers were there without their partners' knowledge so they wouldn't speak to the police – they couldn't. The same atmosphere of reticence prevailed in the other dance halls – the Majestic, the Plaza, the Albert and the Locarno. Jeannie went with the detectives in the hope she would spot her sister's killer but he had disappeared.

Had there really been too much emphasis placed on the one witness, Jeannie Williams? It has been proved that witnesses' recollections are not always as accurate as they had thought. there are many factors that contribute to their inaccuracies, such as a few drinks, the exciting atmosphere of a crowded dance hall, or in this case, the shock of a sister's murder. Jeannie's observations were nonetheless

important; she was sharp and she was able to give many details about 'Bible John'. But had some details to do with height and the overlapping front teeth been confused? Had Jeannie got some of the details of her own dancing partner's appearance mixed up with the appearance of 'Bible John', who had spent the evening dancing with her sister?

The Bible lay open on the table where he had placed it. he had hardly moved from his room and he had heard the comings and goings of the other tenants over the days. The scratch below his eye had healed and his moustache had grown back in. Donning his glasses, he sat down at the table to resume his study of the Bible. He was adept at lying low so the prospect of another few days indoors wouldn't trouble him unduly, as he knew that the hue and cry was ebbing with each day that passed. He had deliberately avoided contact with the other tenants since moving in. They were mostly students who he knew would leave early and return late so that contact with them was almost nil. He had his reasons for this secret privacy. He turned the pages of his Bible to the Book of Numbers, to chapter five, and re-read how the unclean are removed out of the camp, and then went on to chapter 35 where he re-read again about the laws of murder. His finger paused at verse 25: *And the congregation shall deliver the slayer out of the hand of the revenger of blood, and the congregation shall restore him to the city of his refuge, whither he was fled: he shall abide in it unto the death of the High Priest.*

The elderly minister of the Pentecostal Church had admired John X's religious convictions, unaware of his secret double life. A bachelor, he had spent his life in the ministry and was comfortable financially. When he retired at a good age in the early seventies, he moved to the north-east of Scotland but before leaving he had indicated that on his

death John X could expect to benefit from his will. John X visited him at his home on several occasions but something must have happened to cause the old minister to change his mind, because he cancelled the promise he had made earlier. Was this old man in fact the minister who had told John X that there is good cause to believe that murder can be forgiven; and on the strength of his conviction that this claim was a fact, did John X confide in him about the murder? Maybe the minister had his own suspicions of John X? It will never be known why this old man changed his will away from John X's favour. He died in 1976. With the High Priest now dead 'Bible John' was free to strike again.

Did 1977 mark the resumption of 'Bible John's' murderous crusade, begun in the sixties? Five young women were murdered in 1977, the first in August, the second in October. If 'Bible John' was indeed the perpetrator, had he chosen august and October intentionally in order that the police would know he was 'back in business'? Jemima McDonald had been murdered in August 1969 and Helen Puttock in October 1969. Were the cryptic clues being laid again? In 1978 there was one unsolved murder in Dundee in 1979 and a second one, also unsolved, in the same city in 1980; eight unsolved murders of young women all in the space of three years. Could this have been 'Bible John' conducting his crusade with a vengeance, to make up for lost time?

The hunt spread throughout Britain but despite the massive number of hours devoted to the enquiries, the frankly baffled police came no nearer to finding the murderer and what little trail there had been petered out. The pattern had been the same throughout – young women who had been to dance venues had been callously murdered. there were no banner headlines for these latter murders

proclaiming '"Bible John" strikes again!'. had he been forgotten? Senior detectives from Strathclyde, Tayside, Grampian and Lothian police held a high-level conference to discuss the series of unsolved murders and to correlate information.

The murders finally stopped.

But why? One of the strangest aspects of the very strange 'Bible John' story is the sudden appearance and equally sudden end of his deadly works.

His urge to kill was so overwhelming he had to yield to it. Why did he suddenly stop? Or did he? There were the murders in the late seventies in Glasgow and in other parts of Scotland that remain unsolved. It is also possible that 'Bible John' cold have 'grown out' of his murderous tendencies, no longer driven by the compulsion to kill.

There are, of course, other theories which the police considered. As one high-ranking police officer put it: 'There was no such person as "Bible John",' He believes that the murders could have been the work of different people – and, of course, it is not unknown for 'copy-cat' killers to strike and try to throw all the blame on to the first culprit. Could the murders have been the work of 'copy-cat' killers?

There are so many possibilities but the consensus of opinion tends to come down on the 'one-killer' theory. What is certain, despite the detailed descriptions and evidence that the police had, is that the killer of each of these women was clever enough to elude one of the biggest dragnets ever cast in this country. There is very little hope of bringing him to justice unless something – something he reads in his Bible perhaps or the information compiled in this book – prompts him to come forward and come clean.

But there is another explanation as to why the murders stopped. It is in John X's underlining of verses in his study

of the Bible. In Hebrews chapter nine, he highlighted several passages on blood. This chapter deals with the description of the rites and bloody sacrifices of the law. I believe that his interpretation of these passages resulted in the onslaught of murder and that this onslaught ended with his underlining of chapter 10, verse 26: *For if we sin wilfully after that we have received the knowledge of the truth, there remaineth no more sacrifice for sin.* This part of the Bible had more underlining of verses than any other. Significantly, in the same chapter he underlined verse 12 which states: *But this man, after he had offered one sacrifice for sins for ever, sat down on the right hand of God.*

Once more John X thumbed through his Bible and taking up his pen he underlined the verse, *O sing unto the Lord a new song for He hath done marvellous things: His right hand and His holy arm hath gotten Him Victory.* Beside that verse he wrote, 'Dundee 1979–1980'. His cryptic diary/Bible was complete. His victory had been to murder and to elude capture.

To quote a leading psychiatrist: 'He will still be fully aware of what he has done in the past and will be carrying with him the terrible guilt and shame of it. But his

conscience will not be strong enough to make him confess, although he will no longer have the urge to kill again.'

The victims were young women who were enjoying life, only to die at the hands of a religious madman and sadistic murderer. It is all so long ago since he claimed his first victim and his last. They are the forgotten ones. And what of that pleasant guy next door? Think again! How about the nice man who'd had too much to drink when you helped him home? Beware! He is still among us!

POWER IN THE BLOOD

*See therefore, and take knowledge of all hiding places
where he hideth himself, and come ye again with the
certainty, and I will go with you: and it shall come to pass,
if he be in the land I will search him out*
       (SAMUEL, CHAPTER 23, VERSE 23).

AMEN

BIBLIOGRAPHY

Charles N. Stoddart, *Bible John the Sadistic Murderer* (Paul Harris)

Moira Martingale, *Cannibal Killers – the Impossible Monsters* (Hodder and Stoughton)

Richard Wilson, *Scotland's Unsolved Mysteries of the Twentieth Century* (Robert Hale)

William Muncie, *The Crime Pond* (W. & R. Chambers)

Brian McConnell, *The Holy Killers* (Headline)

R.P. Brittain, *The Sadistic Murderer* (Medicine, Science & The Law)

Andrew O'Hagen, *The Missing* (????)